AF293159

 tredition®

tredition was established in 2006 by Sandra Latusseck and Soenke Schulz. Based in Hamburg, Germany, tredition offers publishing solutions to authors and publishing houses, combined with world-wide distribution of printed and digital book content. tredition is uniquely positioned to enable authors and publishing houses to create books on their own terms and without conventional manufacturing risks.

For more information please visit: www.tredition.com

TREDITION CLASSICS

This book is part of the TREDITION CLASSICS series. The creators of this series are united by passion for literature and driven by the intention of making all public domain books available in printed format again - worldwide. Most TREDITION CLASSICS titles have been out of print and off the bookstore shelves for decades. At tredition we believe that a great book never goes out of style and that its value is eternal. Several mostly non-profit literature projects provide content to tredition. To support their good work, tredition donates a portion of the proceeds from each sold copy. As a reader of a TREDITION CLASSICS book, you support our mission to save many of the amazing works of world literature from oblivion. See all available books at www.tredition.com.

Project Gutenberg

The content for this book has been graciously provided by Project Gutenberg. Project Gutenberg is a non-profit organization founded by Michael Hart in 1971 at the University of Illinois. The mission of Project Gutenberg is simple: To encourage the creation and distribution of eBooks. Project Gutenberg is the first and largest collection of public domain eBooks.

A Letter to Dion

Bernard Mandeville

Imprint

This book is part of TREDITION CLASSICS

Author: Bernard Mandeville
Cover design: Buchgut, Berlin – Germany

Publisher: tredition GmbH, Hamburg - Germany
ISBN: 978-3-8472-1322-2

www.tredition.com
www.tredition.de

The Augustan Reprint Society

BERNARD MANDEVILLE

A Letter to Dion

(1732)

With an Introduction by
Jacob Viner

Publication Number 41

Los Angeles
William Andrews Clark Memorial Library
University of California
1953

INTRODUCTION

The *Letter to Dion*, Mandeville's last publication, was, in form, a reply to Bishop Berkeley's *Alciphron: or, the Minute Philosopher*. In *Alciphron*, a series of dialogues directed against "free thinkers" in general, Dion is the presiding host and Alciphron and Lysicles are the expositors of objectionable doctrines. Mandeville's *Fable of the Bees* is attacked in the Second Dialogue, where Lysicles expounds some Mandevillian views but is theologically an atheist, politically a revolutionary, and socially a leveller. In the *Letter to Dion*, however, Mandeville assumes that Berkeley is charging him with all of these views, and accuses Berkeley of unfairness and misrepresentation.

Neither *Alciphron* nor the *Letter to Dion* caused much of a stir. The *Letter* never had a second edition,[1] and is now exceedingly scarce. The significance of the *Letter* would be minor if it were confined to its role in the exchange between Berkeley and Mandeville.[2] Berkeley had more sinners in mind than Mandeville, and Mandeville more critics than Berkeley. Berkeley, however, mere than any other critic seems to have gotten under Mandeville's skin, perhaps because Berkeley alone made effective use against him of his own weapons of satire and ridicule.[3]

Berkeley came to closest grips with *The Fable of the Bees* when he rejected Mandeville's grim picture of human nature, and when he met Mandeville's eulogy of luxury by the argument that expenditures on luxuries were no better support of employment than equivalent spending on charity to the poor or than the more lasting life which would result from avoidance of luxury.[4]

Of the few contemporary notices of the *Letter to Dion*, the most important was by John, Lord Hervey. Hervey charged both Berkeley and Mandeville with unfairness, but aimed most of his criticism at Berkeley. He claimed that *Alciphron* displayed the weaknesses of argument in dialogue form, that it tended either to state the opponent's case so strongly that it became difficult afterwards to refute it or so weakly that it was not worth answering. He found fault with Berkeley for denying that Mandeville had told a great many disagreeable truths—presumably about human nature and its mode of operation in society—and with Mandeville for having told them in public. He held, I believe rightly, that Mandeville, in associating vice with prosperity, deliberately blurred the distinction between vice as an incidental consequence of prosperity and vice as its cause: vice, said Hervey, "is the child of Prosperity, but not the Parent; and ... the Vices which grow upon a flourishing People, are not the Means by which they become so."[5]

T. E. Jessop, in his introduction to his edition of *Alciphron*, characterizes Berkeley's account of the argument of *The Fable of the Bees* as "not unfair," and says: "I can see no reason for whitewashing Mandeville. The content and manner of his writing invite retort rather than argument. Berkeley gives both, in the most sparkling of his dialogues. Mandeville wrote a feeble reply, A *Letter to Dion*."[6] F. B. Kaye, on the other hand, says of the exchange between Berkeley and Mandeville that "men like ... Berkeley, who may be termed the religious-minded ... in their anguish, threw logic to the winds, and criticized him [i.e., Mandeville] for the most inconsistent reasons."[7]

Objective appraisal of the outcome of the debate between Berkeley and Mandeville would presumably lead to a verdict somewhere between those rendered, with appropriate loyalty to their authors, by their respective editors. It is mainly for other reasons, however, that the *Letter to Dion* is still of interest. There is first its literary merit. More important, the *Letter* presents in more emphatic and sharper form than elsewhere two essential elements of Mandeville's system of thought, the advocacy, real or pretended, of unqualified rigorism in morals, and the stress on the role of the State, of the "skilful Politician," in evoking a flourishing society out of the operations of a community of selfish rogues and sinners. The remainder of this introduction will be confined to comments on these two aspects of Mandeville's doctrine. Since the publication in 1924 of F. B. Kaye's magnificent edition of *The Fable of the Bees*, no one can deal seriously with Mandeville's thought without heavy reliance on it, even when, as is the case here, there is disagreement with Kaye's interpretation of Mandeville's position.

It was Mandeville's central thesis, expressed by the motto, "Private Vices, Publick Benefits," of *The Fable of the Bees*, that the attainment of temporal prosperity has both as prerequisite and as inevitable consequence types of human behavior which fail to meet the requirements of Christian morality and therefore are "vices." He confined "the Name of Virtue to every Performance, by which Man, contrary to the impulse of Nature, should endeavour the Benefit of others, or the Conquest of his own Passions out of a Rational Ambition of being good."[8] If "out of a Rational Ambition of being good" be understood to mean out of "charity" in its theological sense of conscious love of God, this definition of virtue is in strict conformity to Augustinian rigorism as expounded from the sixteenth century on by Calvinists and, in the Catholic Church, by Baius, Jansenius, the Jansenists, and others. Mandeville professes also the extreme rigorist doctrine that whatever is not virtue is vice: in Augustinian terms, *aut caritas aut cupiditas*. Man must therefore choose between temporal prosperity and virtue, and Mandeville insists, especially in the *Letter to Dion*, that on his part the choice is always of virtue:

... the Kingdom of Christ is not of this World, and ... the last-named is the very Thing a true Christian ought to renounce. (p. 18)[9]

"Tho' I have shewn the Way to Worldly Greatness, I have, without Hesitation, preferr'd the Road that leads to Virtue." (p. 31)

Kaye concedes: that Mandeville's rigorism "was merely verbal and superficial, and that he would much regret it if the world were run according to rigoristic morality;" that "emotionally" and "practically, if not always theoretically," Mandeville chooses the "utilitarian" side of the dilemma between virtue and prosperity; and that "Mandeville's philosophy, indeed, forms a complete whole without the extraneous rigorism."[10] Kaye nevertheless insists that Mandeville's rigorism was sincere, and that it is necessary so to accept it to understand him. It seems to me, on the contrary, that if Mandeville's rigorism were sincere, the whole satirical structure of his argument, its provocative tone, its obvious fun-making gusto, would be incomprehensible, and there would be manifest inconsistency between his satirical purposes and his procedures as a writer.

Kaye argues that rigorism was not so unusual as of itself to justify doubt as to its genuineness in the case of Mandeville; rigorism was "a contemporary point of view both popular and respected, a viewpoint not yet extinct." To show that rigorism was "the respectable orthodox position for both Catholics and Protestants," Kaya cites as rigorists, in addition to Bayle, St. Augustine, Luther, Calvin, Daniel

Dyke (the author of *Mystery of Selfe-Deceiving*, 1642), Thomas Fuller (1608-1661), William Law, and three Continental moralists, Esprit and Pascal, Jansenists, and J. F. Bernard, a French Calvinist.[11]

Christian rigorism by Mandeville's time had had a long history. From and including St. Augustine on, it had undergone many types of doctrinal dilution and moderation even on the part of some of its most ardent exponents. In Mandeville, and in Kaye, it is presented only in its barest and starkest form. Kaye, however, required by his thesis to show that Mandeville's doctrine was "in accord with a great body of contemporary theory,"[12] while accepting it as "the code of rigorism" treats it as if it were identical with any moral system calling for any measure of self-discipline or associated with any type of religious-mindedness.[13] He also identifies it with rationalism in ethics as such, as if any rationalistic ethics, merely because it calls for some measure of discipline of the passions by "reason," is *ipso facto* "rigorist."[14]

Mandeville was presumably directing his satire primarily at contemporary Englishmen, not at men who had been dead for generations nor at participants in Continental theological controversies without real counterpart in England, at least since the Restoration. If this is accepted, then of the men cited by Kaye to show the orthodoxy and the contemporaneity of rigorism only William Law has any relevance. But Law was an avowed "enthusiast," and in the England of Mandeville's time this was almost as heretical as to be an avowed sceptic. Calvinism in its origins had been unquestionably — though not unqualifiedly — rigoristic. By Mandeville's time, however, avowed Calvinism was almost extinct in England; even in Geneva, in Scotland, in Holland, its rigorism had been much softened by the spread of Arminianism and by a variety of procedures of theological accommodation or mediation between the life of grace and the life of this sinful world. On the Continent, Jansenists were still expounding a severe rigorism. But Jansenist rigorism was not "orthodox." Though not as extreme as Mandeville's rigorism, it had repeatedly been condemned by Catholic authorities as *"rigorisme outré."*[15]

To take seriously Mandeville's rigorism, the narrowness with which he defines "virtue," the broadness with which he defines "vice," his failure to recognize any intermediate ground between "virtue" and outright "vice," or any shades or degrees of either, the positiveness with which he assigns to eternal damnation all who depart in any degree from "virtue" as he defines it, is therefore to accept Mandeville as a genuine exponent of a rigorism too austere and too grim not only for the ordinary run of orthodox Anglicans or Catholics of his time but even for St. Augustine (at times), for the Calvinists, and for the Jansenists.

Kaye justifiably puts great stress on the extent of Mandeville's indebtedness to Pierre Bayle. There is not the space here to elaborate, but it could be shown, I believe, that Mandeville was also indebted greatly, both indirectly through Bayle and directly, to the Jansenist, Pierre Nicole, and that Mandeville's rigorism was a gross distortion of, while Bayle's was essentially faithful to, Nicole's system.[16] Nicole insisted that "true virtue" in the rigorist sense was necessary for salvation, but at the same time expounded the usefulness for society of behavior which theologically was "sinful." But it was the "sinful" behavior of *honnêtes hommes*, of citizens conforming to the prevalent moral standards of their class, not of rogues and rascals, which Nicole conceded to be socially useful.[17] Mandeville, on the other hand, not only lumped the respectable citizens with the rogues and rascals, but it was the usefulness for society of the vices of the rogues and rascals more than—and rather than—those of honest and respectable citizens which he emphasized. In the flourishing hive, prior to its reform, there were:

> ... Sharpers, Parasites, Pimps, Players,
>
> Pick-pockets, Coiners, Quacks, South-sayers,
>
> These were call'd Knaves, but bar the Name,
>
> The grave Industrious were the same.[18]

The moral reform which brought disaster to the "Grumbling Hive" consisted merely in abandonment of roguery and adoption of the standards of the *honnête homme*.[19]

The contrast between his general argument and that of Nicole or Bayle throws light on the role which Mandeville's professed rigorism played in the execution of his satirical purposes. It not only supports the view of all his contemporaries that Mandeville's rigorism was a sham, but also the view that he was not averse to having its insincerity be generally detected, provided only that it should not be subject to clear and unambiguous demonstration. By lumping together the "vices" of the knave and the honest man, Mandeville could without serious risk of civil or ecclesiastical penalties make rigorism of any degree seem ridiculous and thus provide abundant amusement for himself and for like-minded readers; he could then proceed to undermine all the really important systems of morality of his time by applying more exacting standards than they could meet. Against a naturalistic and sentimental system, like Shaftesbury's, he could argue that it rested on an appraisal of human nature too optimistic to be realistic. Against current Anglican systems of morality, if they retained elements of older rigoristic doctrine he could level the charge of hypocrisy, and if they were latitudinarian in their tendencies he could object that they were expounding an "easy Christianity" inconsistent with Holy Writ and with tradition.

Mandeville clearly did not like clergymen, especially hypocritical ones, and there still existed sufficient pulpit rigorism to provide him with an adequate target for satire and a substantial number of readers who would detect and approve the satire. As Fielding's Squire Western said to Parson Supple when the latter reproved him for some misdeed: "At'nt in pulpit now? when art a got up there I never mind what dost say; but I won't be priest-ridden, nor taught how to behave myself by thee." Only if it is read as a satire on rigorist sermons can there be full appreciation of the cleverness of the "parable of small beer" which Mandeville, with obvious contentment with his craftsmanship, reproduces in the *Letter to Dion* (pp. 25-29) from *The Fable of the Bees*. Here the standard rigorist proposition that there is sin both in the lust and in the act of satisfying it is applied to drink, where the thirst and its quenching are both treated as vicious.[20]

Mandeville, as Kaye interprets him, resembles the "*Jansénistes du Salon*" who prided themselves on the fashionable rigor of their doctrine but insisted on the practical impossibility of living up to it in the absence of efficacious grace. In my interpretation, Mandeville was both intellectually and temperamentally a "libertine" patently putting on the mask of rigorism in order to be able at the same time to attack the exponents of austere theological morality from their rear while making a frontal attack on less exacting and more humanistic systems of morality. The phenomenon was not a common one, but it was not unique. Bourdaloue, the great seventeenth-century Jesuit preacher, not very long before had called attention to libertines in France who masqueraded in rigorist clothes in order to deepen the cleavages among the members of the Church: "D'òu il arrive assez souvent, par l'assemblage le plus bizarre et le plus monstrueux, qu'un homme qui ne croit pas en Dieu, se porte pour défenseur du pouvoir invincible de la grâce, et devient à toute outrance le panégyriste de la plus étroite morale."[21]

The *Letter to Dion* has bearing also on another phase of Mandeville's doctrine which is almost universally misinterpreted. Many scholars, including economists who should know better, regard Mandeville as a pioneer expounder of laissez-faire individualism in the economic field and as such as an anticipator of Adam Smith. Kaye accepts this interpretation without argument.

The evidence provided by *The Fable of the Bees* in support of such an interpretation is confined to these facts: Mandeville stressed the importance of self-interest, of individual desires and ambitions, as the driving force of socially useful economic activity; he held that a better allocation of labor among different occupations would result, at least in England, if left to individual determination than if regulated or guided; he rejected some types of sumptuary legislation.

All of this, however, though required for laissez-faire doctrine, was also consistent with mercantilism, at least of the English type. The later exponents of laissez-faire did not invent the "economic man" who pursued only his own interest, but inherited him from the mercantilists and from the doctrine of original sin. English analysis of social process had in this sense always been "individualistic," and in this sense both mercantilism and the widely-prevalent theological utilitarianism were at least as individualistic as later laissez-faire economics. Englishmen, moreover, had long been jealous of governmental power, and at the height of English mercantilism they insisted upon limits to appropriate governmental intervention. It is not safe, therefore, to label anyone before Adam Smith as an exponent of laissez-faire merely on the ground that he would exempt a few specified types of economic activity from interference by government. It would be misleading also to apply to eighteenth-century writers modern ideas as to the dividing line between "interventionists" and exponents of "liberalism" or of "laissez faire." As compared to modern totalitarianism, or even to modern "central economic planning," or to "Keynesianism," the English mercantilism of the late seventeenth and the eighteenth century was essentially libertarian. It is only as compared to Adam Smith, or to English classical and the Continental "liberal" schools of economics of the nineteenth century, that it was interventionist.

Adam Smith is regarded as an exponent of laissez-faire because he laid it down as a general principle (subject in practice to numerous and fairly important specific exceptions) that the activities of government should be limited to the enforcement of justice, to defense, and to public works of a kind inherently unsuitable for private enterprise. He based this doctrine partly on natural rights grounds, partly on the belief that there was a pervasive natural and self-operating harmony, providentially established, between individual interest and the interest of the community, partly on the empirical ground that government was generally inefficient, improvident, and unintelligent.

There is nothing of such doctrine in Mandeville; there is abundant evidence in his writings that Mandeville was a convinced adherent of the prevailing mercantilism of his time. Most English mercantilists disapproved of some or all kinds of sumptuary regulations on the same grounds as Mandeville disapproved of some of them, namely, the existence of more suitable ways of accomplishing their objectives or the mistaken character of their objectives. Mandeville's objection to charity schools on the ground that they would alter for the worse the supplies of labor for different occupations was based on his belief that England, unlike some other countries, already had more tradesmen and skilled artisans than it needed. Mandeville, in contrast to Adam Smith, put great and repeated stress on the importance of the rôle of government in producing a strong and prosperous society, through detailed and systematic regulation of economic activity.

It is a common misinterpretation of Mandeville in this respect to read his motto, "Private Vices, Publick Benefits," as a laissez-faire motto, postulating the natural or spontaneous harmony between individual interests and the public good. The motto as it appeared on title pages of *The Fable of the Bees* was elliptical. In his text, Mandeville repeatedly stated that it was by "the skilful Management of the clever Politician" that private vices could be made to serve the public good, thus ridding the formula of any implication of laissez-faire.

This is made clear beyond reasonable doubt by the *Letter to Dion*. Berkeley, in *Alciphron*, had made Lysicles say: "Leave nature at full freedom to work her own way, find all will be well." Mandeville, taking this as directed against himself, disavows it vigorously, and cites the stress he had put on "laws and governments" in *The Fable of the Bees*. (pp. 3-4; see also 55). He repeats from *The Fable of the Bees* his explanation that when he used as a subtitle the "Private Vices, Publick Benefits" motto, "I understood by it, that Private Vices, by the dexterous Management of a skilful Politician, might be turned into Publick Benefits." (pp. 36-37). Later he refers to the role of the "skilful Management" of the "Legislator" (p. 42), and to "the Wisdom of the Politician, by whose skilful Management the Private Vices of the Worst of Men are made to turn to a Publick Benefit." (p. 45). "They are silly People," he says, "who imagine, that the Good of the Whole is consistent with the Good of every Individual." (p. 49).

A recent work[22] provides indirectly unintentional support to my denial that Mandeville was an exponent of laissez-faire. In this work we are told that "The most famous exponent of what Halévy calls the natural identity of interests is Bernard Mandeville" and that "What Mandeville did for the principle of the natural identity of interests Helvétius did for that of their artificial identity," that is, "that the chief utility of governments consists in their ability to force men to act in their own best interests when they feel disinclined to do so." It so happens, however, that Helvétius as an apostle of state intervention was not only not departing from Mandeville but was echoing him even as to language. Helvétius said that motives of personal temporal interest sufficed for the formation of a good society, provided they were "maniés avec adresse par un législateur habile."[23]

Here also there is a close link between Mandeville, Bayle, and the Jansenists, especially Nicole and Domat. All of them adopted a Hobbesian view of human nature. All of them followed Hobbes in believing that the discipline imposed by positive law and enforced by government was essential if a prosperous and flourishing society was to be derived from communities of individuals vigorously pursuing their self-regarding interests. Mandeville's originality was in pretending that in the interest of true morality he preferred that the individual pursuit of prosperity be abandoned even at the cost of social disaster.

A

LETTER

TO

DION,

Occasion'd by his Book

CALL'D

ALCIPHRON,

OR

The Minute Philosopher.

By the Author of the Fable *of the* Bees.

LONDON:

Printed and Sold by J. Roberts in *Warwick-Lane.*
M.DCC.XXXII.

SIR,

have read your Two Volumes of *Alciphron*, or, The *Minute Philosopher* with Attention. As far as I am a Judge, the Language is very good, the Diction correct, and the Style and whole Manner of Writing are both polite and entertaining: All together bespeak the Author to be a Man of Learning, good Sense and Capacity. My Design in troubling you with this tedious Epistle in Print, which perhaps will be longer than you could have wish'd it, is to rescue the Publick from a vulgar Error, which Thousands of knowing and well-meaning People, and your self, I see, among the Rest, have been led into by a common Report, concerning *The Fable of the Bees*, as if it was a wicked Book, wrote for the Encouragement of Vice, and to debauch the Nation. I beg of you not to imagine, that I intend to blame you, or any other candid Man like your self, for having rashly given Credit to such a Report without further Examination. The *Fable of the Bees* has been presented by a Grand Jury more than once; and there is hardly a Book that has been preach'd and wrote against with greater Vehemence or Severity. When a Work is so generally exclaim'd against, a wise Man, who has no Mind to mispend his Time, has a very good Reason for not reading it. But as your second Dialogue is almost entirely levell'd at that Book and its Author, and you have no where declar'd in Words at length (at least, as I remember) that you never read *The Fable of the Bees*, it is possible I might be ask'd, why I would take it for granted, that you never had read it, when many of your Readers perhaps will believe the contrary. If this Question was put to me, I would readily answer, that I chose to be of that Opinion, because it is the most favourable I can possibly entertain of *Dion*. It is not, Sir, believe me, out of Disrespect, that I call you plain *Dion*; but because I would treat you with the utmost Civility: It is the Name under which, I find, you are pleas'd to disguise your self; and offering to guess at an Author, when he chuses to be conceal'd, is, I think a Rudeness almost equal to that of pulling off a Woman's Mask against her Will.

Whoever reads your second Dialogue, will not find in it any real Quotations from my Book, either stated or examined into, but that the wicked Tenets and vile Assertions there justly exposed, are either such Notions and Sentiments, as first, my Enemies, to render me odious, and afterwards Common Fame had already father'd upon me, tho' not to be met with in any Part of my Book; or else, that they are spiteful Inferences, and invidious Comments, which others before you, without Justness or Necessity, had drawn from and made upon what I had innocently said. I find no Fault with you, Sir; for whilst a Person believes these Accusations against me to be true, and is entirely unacquainted with the Book they point at, it is not impossible that he might inveigh against it without having any Mischief in his Heart, tho' it was the most useful Performance in the World. A Man may be credulous and yet well disposed; but if a Man of Sense and Penetration, who had actually read *The Fable of the Bees*, and with Attention perused every Part of it, should write against it in the same strain, as *Dion* has done in his second Dialogue, then I must confess, I should be at a Loss, what Excuse to make for him.

It is impossible that a Man of the least Probity, whilst he is writing in Behalf of Virtue and the Christian Religion, should commit such an immoral Act as to calumniate his Neighbour, and willfully misrepresent him in the most atrocious Manner. If *Dion* had read *The Fable of the Bees*, he would not have suffer'd such lawless Libertines as *Alciphron* and *Lysicles* to have shelter'd themselves under my Wings; but he would have demonstrated to them, that my Principles differ'd from theirs, as Sunshine does from Darkness. When they boasted of setting Men free, and their abominable Design of ridding them of the Shackles of Laws and Governments, he would have quoted to them the very Beginning of my Preface. *Laws and Government are to the political Bodies of civil Societies, what the vital Spirits and Life it self are to the natural Bodies of animated Creatures.* From the same Preface he would have shew'd those barefaced Advocates for all Manner of Wickedness, the small Encouragement they were like to get from my Book; and as soon as it appear'd, that by Liberty they meant Licentiousness, and a Privilege to commit the most detestable Crimes with Impunity, he would have quoted these Words: *When I assert, that Vices are inseperable from great and potent*

Societies, and that it is impossible, that their Wealth and Grandeur should subsist without; I do not say, that the particular Members of them, who are guilty of any, should not be continually reproved, or not punish'd for them when they grew into Crimes. This he would have corroborated by several Passages in the Book it self, and not have forgot what I say, page 255. *I lay down as a first Principle, that in all Societies, great or small, it is the Duty of every Member of it to be good, that Virtue ought to be encouraged, Vice discountenanc'd, the Laws obey'd, and the Transgressors punish'd.* If he had only read the first Edition, a little Book in Twelves, a Man of *Dion's* Virtue and Integrity could not have stifled the Care I have taken in Fifty Places, nor the many Cautions I have given, that I might not offend or be misunderstood: On the Contrary, he would have made use of them, to undeceive his Friends, and prevented their groundless Fears and senseless Insinuations. If *Dion* had read what I have said about the Fire of *London*, Nothing but his Politeness could have hinder'd him from bursting out into a loud Laughter at the judicious Remark of the Learned *Crito*, where he points at the Probability, that the late Incendiaries had taken the Hint of their Villainies from *The Fable of the Bees*.

I can't say, that there are not several Passages in that Dialogue, which would induce one to believe, that you had dipt into *The Fable of the Bees*; but then to suppose, that upon having only dipt in it, you would have wrote against it as you have done, would be so injurious to your Character, the Character of an honest Man, that I have not Patience to reason upon such an uncharitable Supposition. I know very well, Sir, that I am addressing my self to a Man of Parts, a Master in Logick, and a subtle Metaphysician, not to be imposed upon by Sophistry or false Pretences: Therefore I beg of you, carefully to examine what I have said hitherto, and you'll be convinced; that my not believing you to have read *The Fable of the Bees*, can proceed from Nothing but the good Opinion I have of your Worth and Candour, which I hope I shall never have any Occasion to alter. You are not the first, Sir, by five hundred, who has been very severe upon *The Fable of the Bees* without having ever read it. I have been at Church my self when the Book in Question has been preach'd against with great Warmth by a worthy Divine, who own'd, that he had never seen it; and there are living Witnesses now, Persons of unquestion'd Reputation, who heard it as well as I.

After all, you have advanced Nothing in the second Dialogue concerning me, which it may not be proved to have been said or insinuated over and over in Pamphlets, Sermons and News-Papers of all Sorts and Parties. I can help you to another very good Reason why a Man of Sense might not mistrust the ill Report, that has been spread about *The Fable of the Bees*, and write against it in general Terms, tho' he had not read it. Every body knows, what Pains our Party-writers take in contradicting one another, and that there are few Things, which if the one praises, the other does not condemn. Now, if we find the *London Journal* have a Fling at *The Fable of the Bees* one Day, and *The Craftsman* another, it is a certain Sign that the ill Repute of the Book, must be well establish'd and not to be doubted of. Then why might not an Author write against it, without giving himself the Trouble of reading it? It would be hard, a Man should not dare to affirm, that it is hot in the *East-Indies*, without having made a tedious Voyage thither and felt it. The more therefore I reflect, Sir, on your second Dialogue, and the Manner you treat me in, the more I am convinced, that you never read the Book I speak of, I mean, not read it through, or at least not with Attention. If *Dion* had inform'd himself concerning *The Fable of the Bees*, as he might have done, he must have met with my Vindication of it in some Shape or other. First, it came out in a News-Paper; after that, I publish'd it in a Six-penny Pamphlet, together with the Words of the first Presentment of the Grand Jury and an injurious abusive Letter to Lord C. that came out immediately after it; both which had been the Occasion of my writing that Vindication. The Reason I gave for doing this, was, that the Reader might be fully instructed in the Merits of the Cause between my Adversaries and my Self; and because I thought it requisite, that to judge of my Defence, he should know the whole Charge, and all the Accusations against me at large. I took Care to have this printed in such a Manner, as to the Letter and Form, that for the Benefit of the Buyers, it might conveniently be bound up, and look of a Piece with the then last, which was the second Edition. Ever since the whole Contents of this Pamphlet have been added to the Book, and are at the End of the third, the fourth, and the fifth, as well as this last Impression of 1732. If *Dion* had seen and approved of this Vindication, he would not have wrote against me at all; and if he had thought my Answers not satisfactory, and that I had not clear'd my self from the Aspersions, which had been cast upon me, it was unkind, if not a great Disregard to the Publick, not to take Notice of it, and shew the Insufficiency of my Defence, which from his own Writings it is evident, that great Numbers of the *beau monde* must have acquiesc'd in, or not thought necessary.

Give me Leave, then, Sir, for your own Sake, to treat you, as if you never had read *The Fable of the Bees* and in Return I give you my Word, that I shall make no use of it to your Disadvantage; on the Contrary, I take it for granted, that from the bad Character you had heard of the Book from every Quarter, you had sufficient Reason to write against it, as you have done, without any further Enquiry. This being settled, I shall attempt to shew you the Possibility, that a Book might come into such a general Disrepute without deserving it. An Author, who dares to expose Vice, and the Luxury of the Time he lives in, pulls off the Disguises of artful Men, and examining in to the false Pretences, which are made to Virtue, lays open the Lives of those, *Qui Curios simulant & Bacchanalia vivunt*: An Author, I say, who dares to do this in a great, and opulent, and flourishing Nation, can never fail of drawing upon him a great Number of Enemies. Few Men can bear with Patience, to see those Things detected, which it is their Interest, and they take Pains to conceal. As to Grand Juries, what they go upon is, the Testimony of others; they don't judge of Books from their own Reading; and many have been presented by them, which none, or at least the greatest Part of them had never seen before. Yet when ever the Publisher of a Book is presented by a Grand Jury, it is counted a publick Censure upon the Author, a Disgrace not easily wiped off.

The News-Writers, whose chief Business it is, to fill their Papers and raise the Attention of their Readers, never forget any Scandal which can be publish'd with Impunity. By this Means a Book, which once this Indignity has been put upon, is in a few Days render'd odious, and in less than a Fortnight comes to be infamous throughout the Kingdom without any other Demerit; Those Polemick Authors among them, who are Party-Men, and write either for or against Courts and Ministers, have a greater Regard to what will serve their Purpose, than they have to Truth or Sincerity. As they subsist by vulgar Errors, and are kept alive by the Spirit of Strife and Contention, so it is not their Business to rectify Mistakes in

Opinion, but rather to encrease them when it serves their Turn. They know, that whoever would ingratiate themselves with Multitudes and gain Credit amongst them, must not contradict them; which is the Reason that, how widely soever these Party-Writers may differ from One another in Principles and Sentiments, they will never differ in their Censure or Applause, when they touch upon such Notions which are generally receiv'd.

If you'll consider, Sir, what I have said in the two last Paragraphs, you will easily see the Possibility that Books may get into an ill Repute and a very bad Character without deserving it. The next I shall endeavour to demonstrate to you, is, that this has been the Case of *The Fable of the Bees*, and that the Animosities which have been shewn against it, were originally owing to another Cause, than what my Adversaries pretended to be the true one. In order to this, I shall be obliged to make several Quotations from the Book it self, and repeat many Things, which I have already said in the Vindication hinted at before: But as I design this only for your self and those who have judged of the Book from Common Report, and never perused either the First or the Second Part of it, these Citations will be as new to you as any other Part of my Letter.

I am not ignorant of the Prejudice and real Hurt, which Authors do themselves by making long Quotations. They interrupt the Sense, and often break off the Thread of the Discourse; and many a Reader, when he comes to the End of a long Citation, has forgot the main Subject, and often the Thing it self, which that very Citation was brought in to prove. For this Reason we see, that Judicious Writers avoid them as much as possible; or that where they cannot do without, instead of inserting them in the main Text of their Works, they make Place for them in Notes or Remarks, which they refer to, or else an Appendix, where many of them may be put together, and are never seen but by Choice, and when the Reader is at Leisure. That this segregating all extraneous Matter from the main Body of the Book, the Text it self, is less disagreeable to most Readers, than the other, which I hinted at first, is certain; but it is attended with this ill Consequence, which the less engaging Method of Writing is not, to wit, that many curious and often the most valuable Things, and which it is of the highest Concern to the Author, that they should be known, are neglected and never look'd into, only because they are put into Notes or Appendixes. In my Case you'll find, Sir, that the long Quotations, some of them of several Pages, which I am obliged to trouble you with, are more material for the Vindication of my Book than all that can possibly be said besides. For they will not only demonstrate to you, that I have been shamefully misrepresented, but likewise give you a clear Insight into the real Cause of the Anger, the Hatred, and Inveteracy, of my Enemies, who first gave the Book an ill Name, and were the industrious Authors of the false Reports, by which your self and many other good Men, to my great Affliction, have been impos'd upon. You'll pardon me then, Sir, if, consulting my own Interest in a just Defence, rather than your Pleasure in reading it, I plant my strongest Evidences so directly in your Way, that, if you'll do me the Favour of perusing this Letter, it shall be impossible for you to remain ignorant any longer of the Innocence of my Intentions, and the Injustice that has been done me.

In the Presentment of the Grand Jury in 1723, it is insinuated that in *The Fable of the Bees* there are Encomiums upon Stews, which I can assure you, Sir, is not true. What might have given a Handle to this Charge, must be a Political Dissertation concerning the best Method to guard and preserve Women of Honour and Virtue from the Insults of dissolute Men, whose Passions are often ungovernable. As in this there is a Dilemma between two Evils, which it is impracticable to shun both, so I have treated it with the utmost Caution, and begin thus: *I am far from encouraging Vice, and should think it an unspeakable Felicity for a State, if the Sin of Uncleanness could be utterly banish'd from it; but I am afraid it is impossible.* I give my Reasons, why I think it so; and speaking occasionally of the Musick-Houses at *Amsterdam*, I give a short Account of them, than which Nothing can be more harmless. To prove this to those who have bought or are possess'd of *The Fable of the Bees*, it would be sufficient to appeal and refer to the Book: But as one great Reason of my printing this Letter, is to shew my Innocence to such, who, as well as your self, neither have read nor care to buy the Book, it is requisite I should transcribe the whole. You'll see, Sir, that my Aim is to shew, that these Musick-Houses are discountenanc'd, at the same Time they are tolerated.

In the first Place, the Houses I speak of, are allow'd to be no where but in the most slovenly and unpolish'd Part of the Town, where Seamen and

Strangers of no Repute chiefly lodge and resort. The Street, in which most of them stand, is counted scandalous, and the Infamy is extended to all the Neighbourhood round it. In the Second, they are only Places to meet and bargain in, to make Appointments, in order to promote Interviews of greater Secrecy, and no Manner of Lewdness is ever suffer'd to be transacted in them; which Order is so strictly observ'd, that, bar the Ill Manners and Noise of the Company that frequent them, you'll meet with no more Indecency, and generally less Lasciviousness there, than with us are to seen at a Play-House. Thirdly, the Female Traders, that come to these Evening-Exchanges, are always the Scum of the People, and generally such, as in the Day-Time carry Fruit and other Eatables about in Wheel-barrows. The Habits indeed they appear in at Night, are very different from their ordinaray ones; yet they are commonly so ridiculously gay, that they look more like the Roman Dresses of strolling Actresses, than Gentlewomens Cloaths: If to this you add the Awkwardness, the hard Hands and course Breeding of the Damsels that wear them, there is no great Reason to fear, that many of the better Sort of People will be tempted by them.

The Musick in these Temples of Venus is perform'd by Organs, not out of Respect to the Deity that is worship'd in them, but the Frugality of the Owners, whose Business it is to procure as much Sound for as little Money as they can, and the Policy of the Government, which endeavours as little as is possible, to encourage the Breed of Pipers and Scrapers. All Sea-faring Men, especially the Dutch, are, like the Element they belong to, much given to Loudness and Roaring, and the Noise of Half a Dozen of them, when they call themselves Merry, is sufficient to drown Twice the Number of Flutes or Violins; whereas with one Pair of Organs they can make the whole House ring, and are at no other Charge than the keeping of one scurvy Musician, which can cost them but little, yet notwithstanding the good Rules and strict Discipline that are observ'd in these Markets of Love, the Schout and his Officers are always vexing, mulcting, and, upon the least Complaint, removing the miserable Keepers of them: Which Policy is of two great Uses; First, it gives an Opportunity to a large Parcel of Officers, the Magistrates make use of on many Occasions, and which they could not be without, to squeeze a Living out of the immoderate Gains accruing from the worst of Employments, and at the same Time punish those necessary Profligates, the Bawds and Panders, whom, tho' they abominate, they desire yet not wholly to destroy. Secondly, as on several Accounts it might be dangerous to let the Multitude into the Secret, that those Houses and the Trade that is drove in them are conniv'd at, so, by this Means appear-

ing unblameable, the wary Magistrates preserve themselves in the good Opinion of the weaker Sort of People, who imagine, that the Government is always endeavouring, tho' unable, to suppress what it actually tolerates: Whereas if they had a Mind to rout them out, their Power in the Administration of Justice is so sovereign and extensive, and they know so well how to have it executed, that one Week, nay one Night, might send them all a packing.

I appeal to your self, Sir, whether this Relation is not more proper to give Men (even the Voluptuous, of any Taste) a Disgust and Aversion to the Women in those Houses, than it is to raise any criminal Desire. I am sorry the Grand Jury should conceive, as they said, that I publish'd this with a Design to debauch the Nation; without considering, in the first Place, that there is not a Sentence nor a Syllable, that can either offend the chastest Ear, or sully the Imagination of the most vicious; or, in the Second, that the Matter complain'd of, is manifestly address'd to Magistrates and Politicians, or at least the most serious and thinking Part of Mankind; whereas a general Corruption of Manners, as to Lewdness, to be produced by Reading, can only be apprehended from Obscenities, easily purchased, and every Way adapted to the Tastes and Capacities of the heedless Multitude, and unexperienc'd Youth of both Sexes; but that the Performance so outragiously exclaim'd against was never calculated for either of these Classes of People, is self-evident from every Circumstance. The Beginning of the Prose is altogether Philosophical, and hardly intelligible to any, that have not been used to Matters of Speculation; and the running Title of it is so far from being specious, or inviting, that, without having read the Book it self, No body knows what to make of it, whilst at the same Time the Price is Five Shillings. From all which it is very plain, that if the Book contains any dangerous Tenets, I have not been very sollicitous to scatter them among the People. I have not said a Word to please or engage them, and the greatest Compliment I have made them, has been, *Apage Vulgus. But as Nothing* (I say p 257.) *would more clearly demonstrate the Falsity of my Notions, than that the Generality of the People should fall in with them, so I don't expect the Approbation of the Multitude. I write not to Many, nor seek for any Well-wishers, but among the Few that can think abstractly, and have their Minds elevated above the Vulgar.* Of this I have made no ill Use, and ever preserv'd such a tender Regard to the Publick, that when I have advanced any uncommon Sentiments, I have used all the Precautions imaginable that they might not be hurtful to weak Minds that might casually dip into the Book. When (*page 255*) *I own'd, that it was my Sentiment, that no Society could be raised into a rich and mighty Kingdom, or, so raised, subsist in their Wealth and Power for any considerable Time, without the Vices of Man, I had premised what was true,* that I had *never said or imagin'd, that Man could not be virtuous, as well in a rich and mighty Kingdom, as in the most pitiful Commonwealth;* mind Sir, p. 257. *When I say, that Societies cannot be raised to Wealth and Power and the Top of Earthly Glory without Vices, I don't think, that by so saying, I bid Men be vicious, any more than I bid them be quarrelsome or covetous, when I affirm, that the Profession of the Law could not be maintain'd in such Numbers and Splendour, if there was not Abundance of too selfish and litigious People.* A Caution of the same Nature I had already given towards the End of the Preface, on Account of a palpable Evil, inseparable from the Felicity of *London*. The Words are these, *There are, I believe, few People in London, of those that are at any Time forc'd to go a-foot, but what could wish the Streets of it much cleaner than generally they are, whilst they regard Nothing but their own Cloaths and private Conveniency: but when once they come to consider, that what offends them, is the Result of the Plenty, great Traffick and Opulency of that mighty City, if they have any Concern in its Welfare, they will hardly ever wish to see the Streets of it less dirty. For if we mind the Materials of all Sorts, that must supply such an infinite Number of Trades and Handicrafts as are always going forward, and the vast Quantities of Victuals, Drink, and Fuel, that are daily consumed in it; the Waste and Superfluities, that must be produced from them; the Multitudes of Horses and other Cattle, that are always daubing the Streets; the Carts, Coaches, and more heavy Carriages, that are perpetually wearing and breaking the Pavement of them; and, above all, the numberless Swarms of People, that are continually harassing and trampling through every Part of them: If, I say, we mind all these, we shall find, that every Moment must produce new Filth; and considering how far distant the great Streets are from the River-side, what Cost and Care soever be bestow'd to remove the Nastiness almost as fast as it is made, it is impossible* London *should be more cleanly before it is less flourishing. Now would I ask if a good Citizen, in Consideration of what has been said, might not assert, that dirty Streets are a necessary Evil inseparable from the Felicity of* London, *without being the least Hindrance to the Cleaning of Shoes, or Sweeping of Streets, and consequently without any Prejudice either to the* Blackguard *or the* Scavengers.

But if, without any Regard to the Interest or Happiness of the City, the Question was put, What Place I thought most pleasant to walk in? No body can doubt but before the stinking Streets of London, *I would esteem a fragrant Garden, or shady Grove in the Country. In the same Manner, if, laying aside all worldly Greatness and Vain Glory, I should be ask'd, where I thought it was most probable that Men might enjoy true Happiness, I would prefer a small peaceable Society, in which Men, neither envy'd nor esteem'd by Neighbours, should be contented to live upon the Natural Product of the Spot they inhabit, to a vast Multitude abounding in Wealth and Power, that should always be conquering others by their Arms Abroad, and debauching themselves by Foreign Luxury at Home.*

I own, Sir, it is my Opinion, and I have endeavour'd to prove, that Luxury, tho' depending upon the Vices of Man, is absolutely necessary to render a great Nation formidable, opulent and polite at the same Time. But before you pass any Judgment upon me for this, give me Leave to put you in Mind of Two Things, which I take to be undeniably true. The First is, that the Kingdom of *Christ* is not of this World; and that the last-named is the very Thing a true Christian ought to renounce: I mean, that when we speak of the World in a figurative Sense, as the Knowledge of the World, the Glory of the World; or in *French, Le beau Monde, le grand Monde;* and when in a Man's Praise we say, that he understands the World very well; that, I say, when we use the Word in this Manner, it signifies, and we understand by it that same World which the Gospel gives us so many Cautions and pronounces so severely against. The Second is, that I have wrote in an Age and a Nation, where the greatest Part of the Fashionable, and what we call the better Sort of People, seem to be far more delighted with Temporal, than they are with Spiritual Enjoyments, at the same Time that they profess themselves to be Christians; and that whatever they may talk, preach or write of a Future State and eternal Felicity, they are all closely attach'd to this wicked World; or at least, that the Generality, in their Actions and Endeavours, seem to be infinitely more sollicitous about the one, than they are about the other.

If you will consider these Two Things, you'll find, that I have supposed no Necessity of Vice, but among those by whom worldly Greatness is in Esteem and thought necessary to Happiness. The more curious and operose Manufactures are, the more Hands they

employ; and that with the Variety of them, the Number of Work-
men must still encrease, wants no Proof. It is evident likewise, that
Foreign Traffick consists in changing of Commodities, and removing them from one Place to another. No Nation, that has no Gold or
Silver of their own Growth, can purchase our Product long, unless
we, or Some body else, will buy theirs. The Epithets of polite and
flourishing are never given to Countries, before they are arriv'd at a
considerable Degree of Luxury; and a flourishing Nation without it,
is Bread without Corn, a Perriwig without Hair, or a Library without Books.

Assertions as these, an indulgent Reader will say, might yet be
borne with; and Hypocrites, by putting false Glosses on Things, and
giving favourable Constructions to their Actions, might persuade
the World, that to make this necessary Consumption, they labour'd
for the Publick Good; that they fed on Trouts and Turbots, Quails
and Ortolans, and the most expensive Dishes, not to please their
dainty Palates or their Vanity, but to maintain the Fishmonger and
the Poulterer and the many Wretches, who, for a miserable Live-
lyhood, are daily slaving to furnish them. That they wore gold Bro-
cades, and made new Cloaths every Fortnight, not to gratify their
own Pride or Fickleness, but for the Benefit of the Mercer, the Mer-
chant, and the Weaver, and the Encouragement of Trade in general.
That the Extravagancy of their Tables, and Splendor of Entertainments, were only the Effects of an Hospitable Temper, their Benevo-
lence to others, and a generous Disposition: That Pride or Ostenta-
tion had no Hand in these Things, nor yet in the laying out of the
immense Sums for the Elegancy and Magnificence of Equipages,
Gardens, Furniture and Buildings. All these Things, I dare say, you
would let pass; but if you should hear a Man say, that this Consumption depends chiefly upon Qualities, we pretend to be asham'd
of, it would be offensive to you; and if he should maintain, that,
without the Vices of Man, it would be impossible to enjoy all the
Ease, Glory, and Greatness, the World can afford, and which, in
short, we are fond of, you would think his Assertion to be a terrible
Paradox.

Many People would believe, that Hunger, tho' they never felt the
Extremities of it, is, in order to live, as requisite to a Man, as it is to a
Cormorant, or to a Wolf; and that without Lust, if you give it a soft-

er Name, our Species could not be preserv'd, any more than that of Bulls or Goats. But not One in a Thousand can imagine, tho' it be equally demonstrable, that in the Civil Society the Avarice of Some and the Profuseness of Others, together with the Pride and Envy of most Individuals, are absolutely necessary to raise them to a great and powerful, and, in the Language of the World, polite Nation. It seems still to be a greater Paradox, that natural as well as moral Evil, and the very Calamities we pray against, do not only contribute to this worldly Greatness, but a certain Proportion of them is so necessary to all Nations, that it is not to be conceiv'd, how any Society could subsist upon Earth, exempt from all Evil, both natural and moral.

Yet these Things are asserted, and, I think, demonstrated in *The Fable of the Bees*. The Book has run through several Impressions, and met with innumerable Enemies: Nothing was ever more reviled from the Pulpit as well as the Press. I have been call'd all the ugly Names in Print, that Malice or ill Manners can invent; but not one of my Adversaries has attempted to disprove what I had said, or overthrow any one Argument, I made Use of, otherwise than by exclaiming against it, and saying that it was not true: which to me is a Sign, that not only what I have advanced is not easy to refute, but likewise, that my Opposers are more closely attach'd to the World, than even I my self had imagined them to be. Otherwise it is impossible, but, perceiving this Difficulty, some of them would have reason'd after the following Manner, *viz.* Since this worldly Greatness is not to be attain'd to without the Vices of Man, I will have Nothing to do with it; since it is impossible to serve God and Mammon, my Choice shall be soon made: No temper I Pleasure can be worth running the Risque of being eternally miserable; and, let who will labour to aggrandise the Nation, I will aim at higher Ends, and take Care of my own Soul.

The Moment such a Thought enters into a Man's Head, all the Poison is taken away from the Book, and every Bee has lost his Sting.

Those who should in Reality prefer Spirituals to Temporals, and be seen to take more Pains to attain an everlasting Felicity, than they did for the Enjoyment of the fading Pleasures and transient Glorie of this Life, would not grudge to make some Abatements in the Ease, the Conveniencies, and the Comforts of it, or even to part with some of their Possessions upon Earth, to make sure of their Inheritance in the Kingdom of Heaven. Whatever Liking they might have to the curious Embellishments and elegant Inventions of the Voluptuous, they would refuse to purchase them at the Hazard of Damnation. In Judging of themselves they would not be such easy Casuists, nor think it sufficient not to act contrary to the Laws of the Land, unless they likewise obey'd the Precepts of *Christ*. No Book would be plainer or more intelligible to them than the Gospel; and without consulting either Fathers or Councils, they would be satisfied, that mortifying the Flesh never could signify to indulge every Appetite, not prohibited by an Earthly Legislator.

What Skill, pray, would it require in Controversy, to be convinced, that to yield to all the Allurements, to comply with every Mode and Fashion, and partake of all the Vanities of the World, was the very Reverse of Renouncing it, if Words had any Signification at all? Here lies the Difficulty; and here is the true Cause of the Quarrel, and all the Spite and Invectives against *The Fable of the Bees* and its Author. My Adversaries will not be stinted, or abate an Ace of the wordly Enjoyments they can purchase, because the whole Earth was made for Man; Libertines say the same of Women, and with equal Justice; yet relying on this pitiful Reason, they will eat and drink as deliciously as they can: No Pleasure is denied them, forsooth, that is used with Moderation; and in Cloaths, Houses, Furniture, Equipages and Attendance, they may live in perfect Conformity with the most vain and luxurious of the fashionable People; only with this Difference, that their Hearts must not be attach'd to these Things, and their grand Hope be in Futurity. This notable Proviso being once made, tho' in Words only, all is safe; and no Luxury or Epicurism are so barefac'd, no Ease is so effeminate, no Elegancy so vainly curious, and no Invention so operose or expensive, as to interfere with Religion or any Promises made of Renouncing the World; if they are warranted by Custom, and the Usage of others, who are their Equals in Estate and Dignity.

Oh rare Doctrine! Oh easy Christianity! To be moderate in numberless Extravagancies, *Terence* would tell them was as practicable as *cum ratione insanire*: But if we grant the Possibility of it, how shall we know and be convinced that they are sincere; that their Hearts and Desires are so little engaged to this vile Earth, as they pretend; or that the Thoughts of a World to come are any Part of their real Concern, when we have Nothing but their bare Word for it, and all other Appearances are unanimous, and the most positive Witnesses against them?

I know, that my Enemies won't allow, that I wrote with this View; tho' I have told them before, and demonstrated, that *The Fable of the Bees* was a Book of exalted Morality; they refuse to believe me; their Clamours against it continue; and what I have now said in Defence of it, will be rejected, and call'd an Artifice to come off; that it is full of dangerous, wicked and Atheistical Notions, and could not have been wrote with any other Design than the Encouragement of Vice. Should I ask them what Vices they were; Whoring, Drinking, Gaming; or desire them to name any one Passage, where the least Immorality is recommended, spoke well of, or so much as conniv'd at, they would have Nothing to lay hold on but the Title Page. But why then, will you say, are they so inveterate against it? I have hinted at it just now, but I will more openly unfold that Mystery.

I have, in the Book in Question, exposed the real Pleasures of the Voluptuous, and taken Notice of the great Scarcity of true Self-denial among Christians, and in doing this I have spared the Clergy no more than the Laity: This has highly provoked a great many. But as I have done this without the least Exaggeration, meddled with Nothing, but what is plainly known and seen, and always said less than I could have proved, my Adversaries were obliged to dissemble the Cause of their Anger. What vex'd them the more was, that it was wrote without Rancour or Peevishness; and, if not in a pleasant, at least in an open good-humour'd Manner, free, I dare say, from Pedantry and Sourness. Therefore None of them ever touch'd upon this Point, or spoke one Syllable of the only Thing, which in their Hearts they hate me for.

Here, Sir, I must trouble you with a Parable, in which are couch'd the Prevarications and false Pretences with which the Generality of the World would cover their real Inclinations and the Ends of their Wishes. May it prove as diverting to you as the Matter is really instructive.

In old Heathen Times there was, they say, a Whimsical Country, where the People talked much of Religion; and the greatest Part, as to outward Appearance, seem'd really devout: The chief moral Evil among them was Thirst, and to quench it, a Damnable Sin; yet they unanimously agreed, that Every one was born Thirsty more or less. Small Beer in Moderation was allow'd to All; and he was counted an Hypocrite, a Cynick, or a Madman, who pretended that One could live altogether without it; yet those, who owned they loved it, and drank it to Excess, were counted Wicked. All this while the Beer it self was reckon'd a Blessing from Heaven, and there was no Harm in the Use of it; all the Enormity lay in the Abuse, the Motive of the Heart, that made them drink it. He that took the least Drop of it to quench his Thirst, committed a heinous Crime, whilst others drank large Quantities without any Guilt, so they did it indifferently, and for no other Reason than to mend their Complexion.

They brew'd for other Countries as well as their own; and for the Small Beer they sent abroad, they receiv'd large Returns of Westphaly-Hams, Neats-Tongues, Hung-Beef, and Bolonia-Sausages, Red Herrings, Pickled Sturgeon, Cavear, Anchovies, and every Thing that was proper to make their Liquor go down with Pleasure. Those who kept great Stores of Small Beer by them, without making use of it, were generally envied, and at the same Time very odious to the Publick; and No body was easy that had not enough of it to come to his own Share. The greatest Calamity they thought could befall them, was to keep their Hops and Barley upon their Hands; and the more they yearly consumed of them, the more they reckon'd the Country to flourish.

The Government had made very wise Regulations concerning the Returns that were made for their Exports; encouraged very much the Importation of Salt and Pepper, and laid heavy Duties on every Thing that was not well season'd, and might any ways obstruct the Sale of their own Hops and Barley. Those at Helm, *when they acted in Publick, shew'd themselves on all Accounts exempt and wholly divested from Thirst; made several Laws to prevent the Growth of it, and punish the Wicked who openly dared to quench it. If you examin'd them in their private Persons, and pry'd narrowly into their Lives and Conversations, they seem'd to be more fond, or at least drank larger Draughts of Small Beer than others, but always under Pretence that the Mending of Complexions required greater Quantities of Liquor in them, than it did in those they ruled over; and that what they had chiefly at Heart, without any Regard to themselves, was to pro-*

cure great Plenty of Small Beer among the Subjects in general, and a great Demand for their Hops and Barley.

As No body was debarr'd from Small Beer, the Clergy made use of it as well as the Laity, and some of them very plentifully; yet all of them desired to be thought less Thirsty by their Function than others, and never would own, that they drank any, but to mend their Complexions. In their Religious Assemblies they were more sincere; for as soon as they came there, they all openly confess'd, the Clergy as well as the Laity, from the highest to the lowest, that they were Thirsty; that Mending their Complexions was what they minded the least, and that all their Hearts were set upon Small Beer and Quenching their Thirst, whatever they might pretend to the Contrary. What was remarkable is, that to have laid Hold of those Truths to any one's Prejudice, and made use of those Confessions afterwards out of their Temples, would have been counted very impertinent; and Every body thought it a heinous Affront to be call'd Thirsty, *tho' you had seen him drink Small Beer by whole Gallons. The chief Topicks of their Preachers was the great Evil of Thirst, and the Folly there was in quenching it. They exhorted their Hearers to resist the Temptations of it, inveigh'd against Small Beer, and often told them it was Poyson, if they drank it with Pleasure, or any other Design than to mend their Complexions.*

In their Acknowledgments to the Gods, they thank'd them for the Plenty of comfortable Small Beer they had received from them, notwithstanding they had so little deserv'd it, and continually quench'd their Thirst with it; whereas they were so thorowly satisfy'd, that it was given them for a better Use. Having begg'd Pardon for those Offences, they desired the Gods to lessen their Thirst, and give them Strength to resist the Importunities of it; yet, in the Midst of their sorest Repentance, and most humble Supplications, they never forgot Small Beer, and pray'd that they might continue to have it in great Plenty, with a solemn Promise, that how neglectful soever they might hitherto have been in this Point, they would for the Future not drink a Drop of it with any other Design than to mend their Complexions.

These were standing Petitions, put together to last; and having continued to be made use of without any Alterations for several Hundred Years together, it was thought by Some, that the Gods, who understood Futurity, and knew, that the same Promise they heard in June, *would be made to them the* January *following, did not rely much more on those Vows, than we do on those waggish Inscriptions by which Men offer us their Goods,* To Day for Money, and to Morrow for Nothing. *They often began their Prayers very mystically, and spoke many Things in a spiritual Sense;*

yet they never were so abstract from the World in them, as to end One without beseeching the Gods to bless and prosper the Brewing Trade in all its Branches, and, for the Good of the Whole, more and more to increase the Consumption of the Hops and Barley.

This Parable likewise has been very displeasing to my Enemies, yet they never complain'd of it, nor ever shew'd their Resentment against those Passages, where their Frailties were most exposed. But the true Grievance not being to be named, their next Care was to hinder the Spreading of my Animadversions upon them; that what I had said might not be read by Many; and accordingly, giving the Book an ill Name, and making some imperfect Quotations from it, they procure, as I have said before, the Grand Jury's Presentment against it. But this being now-a-Days the wrongest Way in the World to stifle Books, it made it more known, and encreas'd the Sale of it. This made some hot People raving mad; and now I began to be attack'd with great Fury from all Quarters; but as Nothing has appeared yet, that might not be easily answer'd from *The Fable of the Bees* it self, or the Vindication I have spoke of before, I have not hitherto thought fit to take Notice of any.

It was wrote for the Entertainment of idle People, and calculated for Persons of Education, when they are at Leisure and want Amusement; and therefore to ask Men of Business, or that have any Thing else to do, to read such an incoherent Rhapsody throughout, would be an unreasonable Request; at least, the Author himself ought to be more modest than to expect it: Yet I must beg Leave to say, that whoever has not done this, ought not to be so magisterial in his Censures, as Some have been on Passages the most justifiable in the World. It is impossible to say every Thing at once; and yet Every body, who has a Book before him, has the Liberty of opening and shutting it, when and where he pleases. There are many Things, which we entirely approve of, Part of which we disliked, before we were acquainted with the whole; and we ought always to consider, that Authors often reserve some Places on Purpose to clear up and explain others, that are difficult and obscure: Even when we meet with a Thing really offensive and no ways to be maintain'd, unless we read a Book through, we do not know but the Author has excepted against that very Passage himself; perhaps he has retracted, or begg'd Pardon for it.

It is hardly possible, that a Man of Candour and any tolerable Judgment, who seriously considers the Book, can be offended at it. In the First Place, he will find, that what I call Vices are the Fashionable Ways of Living, the Manners of the Age, that are often practis'd and preach'd against by the same People: Those Vices, that the Persons who are guilty of them, are angry with me for calling them so: The Decencies and Conveniencies, which my Adversaries are so fond of, and which, rather than forsake and part with, they would take Pains to justify. In the Second, That I address myself to the Voluptuous, whose greatest Delight is in this World; and, that when I speak to Others, that would be contented without Superfluities, and prefer Virtue and Honesty to Pomp and Greatness, I lay down quite different Maxims: That what I have said, Page 258, is true, *viz.* Tho' I have shewn the Way to Worldly Greatness, I have, without Hesitation, preferr'd the Road that leads to Virtue.

Should it be objected, that I was not in Earnest, when I recommended those mortifying Maxims, I would answer, That those, who think so, would have said the same to St. *Paul*, or Jesus Christ himself, if he had bid them sell their Estates and give their Money to the Poor. Poverty and Self-denial have no Allurements in Sight of my Enemies; they hate the Aspect and the very Thoughts of them, as much as they do me; and therefore, whoever recommends them must be in Jest. No Mathematical Demonstration is more true, than that to prohibit Navigation, and all Commerce with Strangers, is the most effectual Way to keep out Vice and Luxury: It is almost as true, that Citizens, and Men of Worth, who defend their own, and fight *pro Aris & Focis*, when once disciplin'd and inur'd to Hardship, are more to be depended upon than hired Troops and mercenary Soldiers. Let a Man preach this in *London*, and they'll say he is craz'd. But if Men won't buy Virtue at the Price it is only to be had at, Whose Fault is that?

I knew what People I had to deal with; and when I spoke of the *Spartans* and their Frugality, and how formidable they were to their Enemies, I said then, that such a Way of Living, and a Glory to be obtain'd by so austere a Self-denial, were not the Things which Englishmen wanted or desired. There are Twenty Passages in the Book to the same Purpose; but from this alone it is manifest, that, unless I was a Fool, or a Madman, I could have no Design to encourage or promote the Vices of the Age. It will be difficult to shew me an Author, that has exposed and ridicul'd them more openly. Breaches of the Law I have treated in a more serious Manner; and tho' it has been insinuated, that I was an Advocate for all Wickedness and Villany in General, there is no such Thing in the Book. I have said indeed, that we often saw an evident Good spring up from a palpable Evil, and given Instances to prove, that, by the wonderful Direction of unsearchable Providence, Robbers, Murderers, and the worst of Malefactors were sometimes made instrumental to great Deliverances in Distress, and remarkable Blessings, which God wrought and conferr'd on the Innocent and Industrious; but as to the Crimes themselves, I have never spoke of them, but with the utmost Detestation, and on all Occasions urg'd the great Necessity of punishing all, that are guilty of them, without Favour or Connivance.

That Honesty is the best Policy, even as to Temporals, is generally true; but it does not so often raise Men to great Wealth and Power as Knavery and Ambition; and Opportunity is a great Rascal. Attorneys, Money-Scriveners, Bankers and Brokers, as well as Factors of all Sorts, may, without doubt, be as honest in their Callings as Men of any other; but it is evident in all Trades, that the greater the Trust is to be reposed in Persons, and the more their Transactions are Secrets and such as they can only be accountable for to God and their Conscience, the more Latitude they have of being Knaves without being discover'd. Should now a Man of a Business, where he has great Opportunity of defrauding others with Impunity, be a cunning Sharper, a covetous Miser, and a wicked Hypocrite; can it be a Question, whether he is not more likely to get a great Estate, with the same setting out in a few Years, than a charitable, religious Man, whose chief Care is not for this World, in the same or any other Calling, equally beneficial to fair Dealers? I am not ignorant of what may be said against me, about God's Blessing, and on whom it is most likely to fall. The Dispositions of Providence are unfathomable, and the Distribution of what we call Good and Evil in this World, is a Mystery not to be accounted for by the Notions we have of God's Justice, without having Recourse to a Future State; therefore I need not to take this in Consideration here. The Question is not, which is the readiest Way to Riches, but whether the Riches themselves are worth being damn'd for.

There never was yet, and it is impossible to conceive, an opulent Nation, without great Vices: This is a Truth; and I am not accessary to its being so, for divulging it. When I have shewn the Necessity of Vice, to render a Society great and potent, I have exposed that Greatness, and left it to them, the Members of it, whether it is worth buying at that Price; and I defy all my Enemies to shew me, where I have recommended Vice, or said the least Tittle, by which I contradict that true, as well as remarkable Saying of Monsieur *Baile*. *Les utilités du vice n'empêchent pas qu' il ne soit mauvais*. Vice is always bad, whatever Benefit we may receive from it. — But I have been strangely treated.

Should a thriving Youth in Athletick Health, almost arriv'd at Manhood, industriously waste his Flesh for no other Purpose, than to weigh less, I would 'count him a Fool for his Pains; because he runs the Risque of doing himself great Injury. But he must ride; the Match is made; he has a Master to oblige, and he is undone it he refuses: So he is managed accordingly against the Time. If I had a Mind to expose this Practice, and, laying open the whole Regimen Men are to go through in order to waste, acquaint the World with the sharp Liquors they take, how they are purged, sweated, stinted in their Food, and debarr'd from their natural Rest; If, I say, I had a Mind to do this, and ridicule the Expedient, I don't see where would be the Harm. As to the Thing it self, No body would doubt, but drinking Vinegar, Physicking, Watching, and Starving, would be a more proper Means to lose Flesh, than good Nourishment three Times a Day, and comfortable Sleep at Night. But the Question is, whether Weighing less, or the Riding it self, be of that Importance, that a Man would undergo so much for it; and I believe, most People, far from following this Method, would content themselves with admiring and laughing at the Folly of it. But it would be barbarous to say, that I had prescrib'd it, when I had openly declared against it. But what Name would you give it, if the Jockeys themselves, continuing their former Practice, should in Revenge, that I had expos'd it, pretend seriously to exclaim against me for broaching a destructive Doctrine, that would endanger the Health, and spoil the Growth of young People, and to prove their Assertions, quote as many of my own Words as would serve their Purpose, and no more?

I take this to be a pretty near Resemblance of my Case: *Omne Simile claudicat.* But it is not sufficient for me to say, that I am innocent, any more than it is for my Enemies to cry out, that I am guilty: Men of Sense can not be long imposed upon by either: It is the Book we must stand or fall by at last; and it is to this I refer all judicious as well as impartial Readers. They will soon find out the true Cause of the Malice, and all the Clamours against me, and that my laying open the luxurious Lives of some Men; my shewing the great Scarcity of Self-denial among Christians as well as others, and, in short, my reprehending, lashing and ridiculing Vice and Insincerity, have procured me infinitely more Enemies than all the pretended Encouragement to Vice and Immorality they can meet with; and if, after perusing the whole, all Persons of Candour, and Capacity to read Books of that Nature, are not fully convinced of this, may I be despised for ever, and forfeit the good Opinion of all Men I value. But still the Title, *Private Vices, Publick Benefits*: The hearing and seeing of it, I shall be told, must be offensive to those, who don't read the Book, and will never vouchsafe to look into it.

Pray, Sir, let us examine this. It is evident, that the Words *Private Vices, Publick Benefits* make not a compleat Sentence according to Grammar; and that there is at least a Verb, if not a great deal more wanting to make the Sense perfect. In the Vindication of *The Fable of the Bees*, I have said, that I understood by it, that *Private Vices*, by the dexterous Management of a skilful Politician, might be turn'd into *Publick Benefits.* There is Nothing forc'd or unnatural in this Explanation; and Everybody ought to have the Liberty of being an Interpreter of his own Words. But if I wave this Privilege, the worst Construction that can be put upon the Words is, that they are an Epitome of what I have labour'd to prove throughout the Book, that Luxury and the Vices of Man, under the Regulations and Restrictions laid down in the *Fable of the Bees*, are subservient to, and even inseparable from the Earthly Felicity of the Civil Society; I mean what is commonly call'd Temporal Happiness, and esteem'd to be such.

As to those who, without reading the Book, may be corrupted by the Sight, or by the bare Sound of the Words *Private Vices, Publick Benefits*, I confess, I don't know what Provision to make for them. People who judge of Books from their Titles, must be often imposed upon. There is neither Blasphemy nor Treason in the Words, and they are far enough from Obscenity: If any Mischief is to be fear'd from them, *Drink and be Rich*, a Title that has been bawl'd about the Streets, must be far more dangerous. This latter is a direct Precept, a pernicious, as well as deceitful Doctrine, comprised in a full Sentence, wrote in the Imperative Mood. What strange Consequence would it be of, especially among the Poor, if, relying on the Wisdom of this Title, and taking it for wholesome Advice, People should act accordingly, without any further Examination?

The true Reason why I made use of the Title, *Private Vices, Publick Benefits*, I sincerely believe, was to raise Attention: As it is generally counted to be a Paradox, I pitch'd upon it in Hopes that those who might hear or see it, would have the Curiosity to know, what could be said to maintain it; and perhaps sooner buy the Book, than they would have done otherwise. This, to the best of my Knowledge, is all the Meaning I had in it; and I think it must have been Stupidity to have had any other.

If it be urged, that these Benefits are worldly, I own it; and Every body may see, in whose Sense I call them so; in the Language of the World, the Age and the Time I live: This one of my Adversaries perceived plainly, and endeavoured to take Advantage of it against me, by saying, that Nothing could be a real Benefit, that did not conduce to a Man's eternal Happiness; and that it was evident, that the Things, to which I gave that Name, did not. I agree with him, that a Man's Salvation is the greatest Benefit he can receive or wish for; and I am persuaded, that, speaking of Things Spiritual, the Word is very proper in that Sense; the same may be said of the Words Profit, Gain, and, if you please, Lucre; but I deny, that without any Addition, this is the common Acceptation of them; in which, I hope, I may have the Liberty to make use of Words with the Rest of my Fellow-Subjects. All temporal Privileges and worldly Advantages whatever, are call'd Benefits, and a Thousand Things are beneficial to the Body, that have Nothing to do with the Soul. So a Felon may have the Benefit of the Clergy; such are Benefit-Tickets; and so a Man may go in the Country for the Benefit of the Air. I would ask this wise Gentleman, when he reads, that a Play is to be acted for the Benefit of such a one; which he thinks it is, the Money the Person receives, or the Performance it self, that contributes most to his eternal Happiness.

But I am more cautious and exact, than my Enemies imagine: If I would have made my Readers to understand, that the Vices of Men often prove of worldly Advantage to those who commit them, tho' it is very true, yet in this Case, I would not have used the Word Benefit in so general a Manner: for as Nothing is of greater Concern to every individual Person, than his future Welfare, Nothing can be Beneficial to him, in an unlimited Sense, that might destroy, or any Ways interfere with his eternal Happiness: But this eternal Happiness cannot at the soonest commence till after this Life; and when a Man is dead, he ceases to be a Member of the Society, and he is no longer a Part of the Publick; which latter is a collective Body of living Creatures, living upon this Earth, and consequently, as such, not capable of enjoying eternal Happiness. A Miser may go directly to Hell, as the Reward of his Avarice and Extortion, at the same Time, that the great Wealth he leaves, and the Hospital he builds, are a considerable Relief to the Poor, and consequently a Publick Benefit.

If a Man should affirm, that the Publick is wholly incapable of having any Religion at all, it would, perhaps, be shocking to some People; yet it is as true, as that the Body Politick, which is but another Name for the Publick, has no Liver nor Kidneys, no real Lungs nor Eyes in a literal Sense. Mix'd Multitudes of Good and Bad Men, high and low Quality, may join in outward Signs of Devotion, and perform together what is call'd Publick Worship; but Religion it self can have no Place but in the Heart of Individuals; and the most a Legislator can act in Behalf of it in a Christian Country, is, first, to establish it by Law; and, after that, every way to secure and promote the Exercise of it on the one Hand; and, on the other, to prohibit and punish Wickedness, and all Manner of Impiety, that can fall under the Cognizance of Magistrates. But thus much I think to be necessary in the Civil Administration of all Governments, for the temporal Interest of the Whole, before true Christianity comes in Question, which is a private Concern of every Individual: And tho' I have not every where taken Notice of this, when I have been soothing the Voluptuous, yet when it has come directly in my Way, I have earnestly recommended to all Magistrates the Care of Divine Worship, even when my greatest Regard has been for the Wealth and Greatness of Nations, and the Advancement of worldly Glory; which good Christians ought to have little to do with. Of which you may see an undeniable Proof in Page 352, where speaking of the Instructions the Children of the Poor might receive at Church; *From which, I say, or some other Place of Worship, I would not have the meanest of the Parish, that is able to walk to it, be absent on Sundays*, I have these Words: *It is the Sabbath, the most useful Day in Seven, that is set apart for Divine Service & Religious Exercise, as well as Resting from bodily Labour; and it is a Duty incumbent on all Magistrates, to take a particular Care of that Day. The Poor more especially, and their Children, should be made to go to Church on it, both in the Fore- and the Afternoon, because they have no Time on any other. By Precept and Example they ought to be encourag'd to it from their Infancy. The wilful Neglect of it ought to be 'counted scandalous; and if down-right Compulsion to what I urge, might seem too harsh, and perhaps impracticable, all Diversions, at least, ought strictly to be prohibited, and the Poor hinder'd from every Amusement abroad, that might allure or draw them from it.*

I return to my Subject. How shocking to Some, and ridiculous to others, the explanatory Part of the Title I mention'd, may have been, yet it is irrefragrably true; and there are various Ways, by which Private Vices may become Publick Benefits, Ways more real and practicable, than what, some Time ago, was offer'd by that serious Divine, whose Religion and Piety are so amply set forth in that un-disguised Confession of his Faith, *The Tale of a Tub*. People may wrangle about the Definition of Luxury as long as they please; but when Men may be furnish'd with all the Necessaries for Life from their own Growth, and yet will send for Superfluities from Foreign Countries, which they might (as many actually do) live comfortably without, it certainly is a Degree of Luxury, if there be such a Thing as Luxury in the World. Now, if a Legislator, who is to take Care of the Welfare, and consequently the Defence, as well as the Tranquili-ty of the Publick, perceiving this vicious Inclination and Longing after Superfluities, made use of it as a Means to provide for the Pub-lick Safety, and actually raised Money by Licensing the Importation of such Foreign Superfluities; might it not be said, that, by such skilful Management, *Private Vices* were turn'd into *Publick Benefits*? And is this not done, when heavy Duties are laid on Sugar, Wine, Silk, Tobacco, and a Hundred other Things less necessary, and not to be purchas'd but with infinite Toil and Trouble, and at the Haz-ard of Men's Lives? If you tell me, that Men may make use of all these Things with Moderation, and consequently that the Desire after them is no Vice, then I answer, that either no Degree of Luxury ought to be call'd a Vice, or, that it is impossible to give a Definition of Luxury, which Every body will allow to be a just one.

But I'll give you another Instance, how palpable and gross Vices may be, and are turn'd into Publick Benefits. It is the Business of all Law-givers to watch over the Publick Welfare, and, in order to procure that, to submit to any Inconveniency, any Evil, to prevent a much greater, if it is impossible to avoid that greater Evil at a cheaper Rate. Thus the Law, taking into Consideration the daily Encrease of Rogues and Villains, has enacted, that if a Felon, before he is convicted himself, will impeach two or more of his Accomplices, or any other Malefactors, so that they are convicted of a Capital Crime, he shall be pardon'd and dismiss'd with a Reward in Money. There is no Doubt but this is a good and wise Law; for without such an Expedient, the Country would swarm with Robbers and Highwaymen Ten-times more than it does; for by this Means we are not only deliver'd from a greater Number of Villains, than we could expect to be from any other; but it likewise stops the Growth of them, breaks their Gangs, and hinders them from trusting One another. For Three Rogues, acting separately, cannot do so much substantial Mischief on all Occasions, as when they act in Company. All this while it is evident, that in this Case the Law has only Regard to the Publick Good, and, to procure that, sets aside all other Laws, and proceeds rather contrary to the Common Notions we have of Justice; which, according to the *Civilians*, consists *in a constant and perpetual Desire of giving every one his Due*: For instead of Hanging, which is a Felon's Due, it pardons him; and for Fear he should have some Goodness left, and that natural Compassion might make him unwilling to destroy his dearest Friends, and perhaps his Brother, with his Breath, the Law invites him to it by a large Sum of Money, and actually bribes him to add to the Rest of his Crimes that Piece of Treachery to his Companions, whom he had sworn Fidelity to, and perhaps drawn into the Villany.

It is in vain to tell me, that this Impeaching of his Companions is no Crime in a Felon, but a Duty which he owes his Country; and that I don't know but it is the Effect of his sincere Repentance, which makes him look upon this open Confession as the only Attonement he is able to make the Publick for all his Offences against it. Those who would impeach Others from a Motive of Conscience, and a Sense of their Duty, were not the Men the Legislature had in View. When that Law was made, it was well known, from what was observed of Thieves, Pickpockets, and House-breakers, that those Common Villains will do any Thing to get Money, and still more to save Life, when they are conscious that it is forfeited. The Knowledge of this was the Foundation of that Law. For the Worst of Rogues have Friendship and Affection for one another; and Constancy, Faithfulness, and Intrepidity are 'counted valuable Qualities among them, as well as among other People. One Villain who betrays another merely for Money, and without Necessity, thinks himself to be guilty of a bad Action; and among the many Hundreds of Rogues, who have impeach'd and hang'd their Companions, I don't believe there ever was one, who made himself a Witness against an Associate, with whom he was not at Enmity before, if he could have got the same Temporal Advantage by holding his Tongue.

This shews the Usefulness of such a Law, and at the same Time the Wisdom of the Politician, by whose skilful Management the Private Vices of the Worst of Men are made to turn to a Publick Benefit. There are Men who are of Opinion, that no positive Evil may be done or commanded, that Good may come of it, on any Account whatever: Should any one of these be in doubt whether there is not some Reasonableness or other Merit in this Law, besides its contributing to the Welfare of the Society; I would ask him, if it would not be an unpardonable Folly, nay a wicked Action in any Legislature, to enact, that a most abandon'd Wretch, who has been guilty of many Capital Crimes, should, without having shewn any Remorse, not only be pardon'd, but likewise with a Reward in Money be let loose again upon the Publick; if what is design'd by such an extraordinary Conduct, to wit, the Decrease of Thefts and Villanies, might be obtain'd by any other Method, less clashing with the common Notions we have of Justice: Which being undeniably true, the only Reason that can be given, why Enacting this is neither Wickedness nor Folly, is Necessity, and the Publick Benefit, which is expected from it.

If All I have said hitherto in Defence of the *Fable of the Bees*, and what I have quoted from it, have not alter'd the Opinion you seem to have had of the Book, I believe it is in vain to say any more: Other Readers, I hope, will be less obdurate, and convinced by this Time, that it was not wrote for the Encouragement of Vice and to debauch the Nation; which is all I want; for as to the Performance, whether good or bad, I shall say Nothing about it, whatever I think. I sincerely believe, Sir, that most Authors (whatever they say to the Contrary) have a better Opinion of their Works than they deserve; and I fancy, that most People believe so too: Therefore whether it is well or ill wrote, as to the Diction, Manner, and whatever regards the Composition, is what I would never have troubled my Head about, tho' it had been more generally condemn'd than it has been.

The Censurers of the Book themselves, who have publickly attack'd it, are not unanimous about the Merit of it; and Two of them, who have both wrote against it by Name, differ very widely in their Opinion concerning this Composition. A noted[24] Critick, who seems to hate all Books that sell, and no other, has, in his Anger at that Circumstance, pronounced against *The Fable of the Bees* in this Manner: *It is a wretched Rhapsody; the Wit of it is low; the Humour of it contemptibly low, and the language often barbarous.* But a Reverend Divine, who has wrote a long Preface against the same Book, seems not to have disliked the Performance of it, nor to wonder at the quick Sale of it, which he ascribes in a great Measure[25] *to the free, easy and lively Manner of the Author.* From this Contrariety of Opinions, I shall infer Nothing more, than that, if Men would be truly inform'd of the Book, it is not safe to trust to the Reports which are spread of it. What Pity it is, you did not know this before you wrote your *Minute Philosopher!*

There are few Men, even among the most able, who can judge of Books impartially. We are often influenc'd by our Love, or our Hatred, before we are aware of it our selves. I have met with several good Judges of Books, who disliked, and spoke very slightingly of your *Alciphron;* and I found, the chief Reason was, because you attack'd all *Free Thinkers,* without Exception. But I declare, that I think your Book, for the Generality, to be well wrote; tho' you have us'd me most unmercifully, and not acted, if you had read *The Fable of the Bees,* like an honest Man. When a Person has a handsome Face, I can't be so stupid as to believe him ugly, because he has us'd me ill. I differ from My Lord *Shaftesbury* entirely, as to the Certainty of the *Pulchrum & Honestum*, abstract from Mode and Custom: I do the same about the Origin of Society, and in many other Things, especially the Reasons why Man is a Sociable Creature, beyond other Animals. I am fully persuaded, His Lordship was in the Wrong in these Things; but this does not blind my Understanding so far, as not to see, that he is a very fine Author, and a much better Writer than my self, or you either. If that noble Lord had been a much worse Author, and wrote on the Side of Orthodoxy and the Church, I fancy, you would have thought more favourably of his Capacity. I have seen what you have cited from him, and the Manner you have done it in. But what Proportion does that bear to Three large Volumes, and the many admirable Things he has said against Priest-craft, and on the Side of Liberty and Human Happiness. Upon the Whole, I dare say, that your *Minute Philosopher* will meet with very few Readers, among those that have read, and are not lash'd in the *Characteristicks*, who will think, that My Lord *Shaftsbury* deserves one Tenth Part of the Indignity and Contempt, which you treat *Cratylus* with.

Men may differ in Opinion, and both mean well. You, Sir, think it for the Good of Society, that human Nature should be extoll'd as much as possible: I think, the real Meanness and Deformity of it to be more instructive. Your Design is, to make Men copy after the beautiful Original, and endeavour to live up to the Dignity of it: Mine is, to enforce the Necessity of Education, and mortify Pride. I was very much delighted with what you say in your First Dialogue of Apple-trees and Oranges; the different Productions of the first, and the Culture of the other. The Allegory is very ingenious, and the Application just; but I don't think, that the Conclusion, which must be drawn from it, will be of great Use to you. Page 51. *Euphranor asks Alciphron, Why may we not conclude by a Parity of Reason, that Things may be natural to Human Kind, and yet neither found in all Men, nor invariably the same, where they are found?* I answer, They may. But if all the Knowledge and Accomplishments, which Men can attain to, are to be look'd upon as natural, and peculiar to the whole Species, it must be the same with Vice and Wickedness, as it is with Virtue and the Liberal Arts; and, what I never could have imagin'd before, it must be as natural for a Man to murder his Father, as it is to reverence him; and for a Woman to poison her Husband, as it is to love him.

If you would but look into the Reasons, Sir, I have given for distinguishing between what is natural, and what is acquired, you would not find any ill Intention in that Practice. Many Things are true, which the Vulgar think Paradoxes. Believe me, Sir, to understand the Nature of Civil Society, requires Study and Experience. Evil is, if not the Basis of it, at least a necessary Ingredient in the Compound; and the temporal Happiness of Some is inseparable from the Misery of others. They are silly People who imagine, that the Good of the Whole is consistent with the Good of every Individual; and the best of us are insincere. Every body exclaims against Luxury; yet there is no Order of Men which is not guilty of it; and if the Lawgivers are not always endeavouring to keep up all Trades and Manufactures, that supply us with the Means and Implements of Luxury, they are blamed. To wish for the Encrease of Trade and Navigation, and the Decrease of Luxury at the same Time, is a Contradiction. For suppose, that the Legislature, by the Help of the Clergy, could introduce a general Frugality in this Nation, we could never keep up our Traffick, and employ the same Hands and Shipping, unless they could likewise persuade the Nations, we deal with, to be more profuse than now they are, that they might take off from our Hands so much more of the Implements of Luxury, as our Consumption of them should be less than it had been before.

The very same Things, which are Blessings in One Year, are Calamities in another. In every Nation, those who are employ'd in Gardening and Agriculture, are taught by Experience to manage their Affairs, as is most suitable to the Climate and the Certainty or Irregularities of the Seasons. If there were no Blasts in *England*, nine Tenths of the Apple-trees would be superfluous. Ask the Gardeners about *London*, whether they don't get more by a middling Crop, than a plentiful Product; and whether Half of them would not be ruin'd, if every Thing they sow or plant should come to Perfection: Yet Every body wishes for Plenty and Cheapness of Provisions: But they are often Calamities to a great Part of the Nation. If the Farmer can't have a reasonable Price for his Corn, he can't pay his Landlord. We have often had the good Fortune of having great Plenty, when other Nations have wanted. This is a real Gain: But when all our

Neighbours are sufficiently provided, and we can no where export our Corn with Profit, Two plentiful Years, one after an other, are a greater Detriment to the Publick by far, than a middling Scarcity. A benevolent Man, who has a favourable Opinion of his Kind, would perhaps imagine, that Labourers of all Sorts would go to their Work with greater Alacrity, and bear the Fatigue of it with more Chearfulness, in plentiful Years, than when Corn is at a high Price, and with all their Industry they can hardly procure Food for their Families. But the Contrary is true; and ask all considerable Dealers, of Experience, who for many Years have employ'd a great Number of Hands in the Woollen Manufacture, in Hard Ware, or Agriculture, and they will tell you unanimously, that the Poor are most insolent, and their Labour is least to be depended upon, when Provisions are very cheap; and that they never can have so much Work done, or their Orders so punctually comply'd with, as when Bread is dear.

Your *Crito* and *Euphranor* are very good Characters; but what I admire the most in them, is the consummate Patience in keeping Company, and bearing for a whole Week together, with two such insupportable, out of the way Rascals, as you have represented *Alciphron* and *Lysicles* to be. I believe with you, that among the Vain and Voluptuous, there are Abundance of superficial People, who call themselves *Free Thinkers*, and are proud of being thought to be Unbelievers, without having laid the Foundation of any Philosophy at all. But there never were Two such Creatures in the World as those whom you have made the Champions for Free-thinking. I don't speak as to their Irreligion and Impiety, or their Incapacity of maintaining what they loudly assert; for such there are many among Rakes and Gamesters. But the Knowledge, good Sense and Penetration, which your Libertines display at some Times, are inconsistent with the Ignorance, Folly and Stupidity they shew at others. It is impossible that Men of Parts, and the least Spirit, how much soever they were in the Wrong, could see themselves defeated, banter'd and exposed with so much Tranquility and Chearfulness; and I can't conceive how any, but egregious Coxcombs, without Sense of Shame, could behave as *Alciphron* and *Lysicles* do throughout your Dialogues. They are Fellows without Feeling or Manners. If among Gentlemen there are abandon'd Wretches, who harbour Sentiments so abominable and openly destructive to Society, as several are which they advance, I am very well assured, that no well-bred Men would vent them before Strangers in so shocking a Manner as they do. No Mortal ever saw such Disputants before; they always begin with swaggering and boasting of what they'll prove; and in every Argument they pretend to maintain, they are laid upon their Backs, and constantly beaten to Pieces, till they have not a Word more to say; and when this has been repeated above half a Score times, they still retain the same Arrogance and *mal-à-pert* Briskness they were made to set out with at first; and immediately after every Defeat, they are making fresh Challenges, seemingly with as much Unconcern and Confidence of Success, as if Nothing had pass'd before, or they remember'd Nothing of what had happened. Such an Undauntedness in assaulting, and Alacrity in yielding, as you have made them display, never met in the same Individuals before.

I know, Sir, that in drawing those Characters, you design'd them for Monsters to be abhorr'd and detested; and in this you have succeeded to Admiration, at least with me; for I can assure you, that I never saw any two Interlocutors in the same Dialogue or Drama, whose Behaviour and Principles I execrate more heartily, than I do theirs. And if you would read the *Fable of the Bees* impartially, you would be convinced of this, from my Description of the Company I would chuse to converse with. Upon, such a Condescension, I would likewise demonstrate to you, how you and I might assist and be useful to one another, as Authors.

You allow, that there are vicious Clergymen, who are unworthy of their Function. I foresee, that Some of these, who have neither *Crito's* Learning, nor *Euphranor's* good Sense, will make use of your *Alciphron* for an evil Purpose. Having by their bad Courses made themselves contemptible to all who know them, they will endeavour to stop the Mouths of all Opposers, by barely naming the *Minute Philosopher*; and having, by the Credit of that Book, repell'd the Censure they had deserv'd, insult the Laity, and lay claim to the Honour and Deference, which ought only to be paid to worthy Divines. These I will take in Hand, and convince, that you have not wrote to justify those Ecclesiasticks, who by their Practice contradict the Doctrine of *Christ*; and that they misconstrued your Intentions; who leading vicious Lives themselves, demanded the same Respect from Others, which you only affirm to be due to Clergymen of Merit and good Morals. And as I would handle these, so you, in like Manner, would take to Task those vile Profligates, who, copying after your Originals, should at any Time endeavour to shelter themselves under my Wings. Should ever a second *Lysicles* pretend to prove, that the more Mischief Men did, the more they acted for the Publick Welfare, because it is said, in *The Fable of the Bees*, that without Vices, no great Nation can be rich and flourishing, you would laugh at his Folly; and if, for the same Reason, he urged, that Rapes, Murder, Theft, and all Manner of Villanies ought to be applauded, or at least pass'd by with Impunity, you would demonstrate to him, how immensly far my Design was from screening Criminals, and shew him the many Passages, where I insist upon it, that impartial Justice ought to be administer'd, and that even for the Welfare of worldly-minded Men, Crimes should be severely punish'd. You would inform him likewise, that I thought Nothing more cruel, than the Lenity of Juries, and the Frequencies of *Pardons*, and not forget to tell him, that my Book contained several Essays on Politicks; that the greatest Part of it was a Philosophical Disquisition into the Force of the Passions, and the Nature of Society, and that they were silly People, who made any other Construction of it.

I observe in your fifth Dialogue, that you think the Multitudes among Christians to have better Morals, than they were possess'd of among the antient Heathens. The Vices of Men have always been so inseparable from great Nations, that it is difficult to determine any Thing with Certainty about that Matter. But I am of Opinion, that the Morals of a People in general, I mean the Virtues and Vices of a whole Nation, are not so much influenced by the Religion that is profess'd among them, as they are by the Laws of the Country, the Administration of Justice, the Politicks of the Rulers, and the Circumstances of the People. Those who imagine, that the Heathens were encouraged and led to criminal Pleasures by the bad Examples of the Deities they worship'd, seem not to distinguish between the Appetites themselves, the strong Passions in our Nature, that prompt Men to Vices, and the Excuses they make for committing them. If the Laws and Government, the Administration of Justice, and the Care of the Magistrates were the same, and the Circumstances of the People were likewise the same, I should be glad to hear a Reason, why there should be more or less Incontinence in *England*, if we were Heathens, than there is, now we are Christians. The real Cause of Fornication, and Adultery, the Root of the Evil, is Lust. This is the Passion, which is so difficult to conquer, whilst it affects us. There are many Christians, no doubt, who subdue it by the Fear of God, and Punishment hereafter; but I believe, that the Heathens, who triumph'd over this Passion, from a Regard to Virtue, were as considerable in Number. Among the nominal Christians, there are not a Few, who forbear indulging this Passion, from worse Principles. I believe it was the same with the Heathens. However, in *Great-Britain* there are Thousands that abstain from unlawful Pleasures, who would not be so cautious, if they were not deterr'd from them by the Expence, the Fear of Diseases, and that of losing their Reputation. These are three Evils, against which all the bad Examples of the Gods can bring no Remedy.

In all Ages, Men have display'd Virtues and Vices, which their Religion had Nothing to do with; and in many Actions, and even the most important Affairs, they are not more influenced by what they believe of a Future State, than they are by the Name of the Street they live in. When People shew great Attachment to the World and their Pleasure, and are very cool, and even neglectful in Religious Duties, it is ridiculous to ascribe their good Qualities to their Christianity. You'll give me Leave, Sir, to expatiate a little upon this Head, and illustrate my Meaning in a Character or two, which I am going to draw.

Lepidus, a Man of good Sense, is a Batchellor, and never intends to marry. He is far from being chast, but cautious in his Amours. He is a Lover of Mirth and Gaiety, hates Solitude, and would rather take up with almost any Company, than be alone. He keeps a very good Table; no Man treats with a better Grace; and seems never to be better pleased, than when he is entertaining his Friends. He has a very great Estate, yet at the Year's End he lays up but little of his large Revenue. Notwithstanding this, he lives within Compass, and would think Nothing more miserable, than not to be rich. He is a Man of Honour, and has a high Value for Reputation. He is of the establish'd Church, and commonly goes to it once every Sunday; but never comes near it at any other Time. Once likewise every Year, either at *Easter* or *Whitsuntide*, he takes the Sacrament. For the

Rest, Pleasure and Politeness are his chief Study: He seems to be little affected with Religion, and seldom speaks of it, either for or against it. Now, if a Man, having well weigh'd and examin'd this Character, was ask'd what he thought of *Lepidus*, as to his Principle, and the Motives of his Actions, and he should give it as his Opinion, that this Sociableness, this generous and *debonnair* Temper of *Lepidus* were owing to his being a Christian, and not a Heathen or a Freethinker, it might be call'd a charitable Construction, but I could never think it well judg'd. But be that as it will, if a *Crito* or an *Euphranor* had a Mind to advance such an Opinion, and stand to it, I am fully persuaded, that it would be easy for them to say so much in Behalf of it; that it would not only be difficult to disprove it, but likewise a very odious Task to set about it.

Nicanor is a very sober Man; hardly ever drinks to Excess; yet he is never without Wine of several Sorts, and is very free with it to his Friends, and all who come to see him. But whatever his Company may do, he always fills very sparingly for himself, and seldom drinks above half a Pint at a Sitting. He never goes to a Tavern but about Business; and when he is alone, Small Beer or Water are the Liquors he chuses. *Nicanor*, who was always an industrious Man, is become rich by his Trade, yet as indefatigable as ever, and seems to know no greater Pleasure than the getting of Money. He is not void of Ambition; is Deputy of the Ward he lives in, and hopes to be an Alderman before he dies. Once in his Life he was drunk, but that was in driving a Bargain, by which he got Five Hundred Pound in one Morning. Let us suppose, that this Character being likewise look'd into, a Man shou'd take it into his Head to affirm, that the Industry and Desire after Wealth of *Nicanor* were owing to his Love of Wine, One would imagine, that it would not be difficult to refute this Man, and to prove, that what he advanced was a wrong Judgment, if not a ridiculous Surmise.

For if *Nicanor* loved Wine, he would drink more of it. He is rich enough to buy it, nay he has Plenty of it, tho' he hardly ever touches it, when he is by himself. He grudges it not to Others; and it is incredible, that if he loved Wine, he should only fill Thimbles full for himself, whilst he saw Others drink Bumpers to his Cost with Pleasure. You will think perhaps, that I have said too much already, to prove a Thing that is as clear as the Sun. But if it was as reputable, and 'counted as necessary to real Happiness to love Wine, as it is to be Religious; and a Man of *Euphranor*'s Capacity had a Mind to be *Nicanor*'s Advocate, and maintain, that the Love of Wine was the Motive of his Industry, in Spight of all the Appearances to the Contrary; if, I say, a Man had a Mind to maintain this, and had *Euphranor*'s Capacity, he might make a great Shew for his Client, without the Learning of *Crito*, and would certainly baffle his Adversaries, if he had such pliable ones as *Alciphron* and *Lysicles* to deal with. Come, would *Euphranor* say, answer me, *Alciphron*; is it not demonstrable, that the more Money a Man has, the more able he is to buy Wine. *Alciphron* would answer, I cannot deny that; and here the Dialogue would begin. *Euphr.* When there are plain Evidences that a Man has been drunk, would you deny it to be true? *Alciph.* I would never speak against Matter of Fact. *Euph.* Would you pretend to prove from a Man's having been drunk, that he does not love Wine? *Alciph.* I own I would not. *Euph.* You, who are a Free Thinker, and have enquir'd so minutely into Human Nature, do you think there is a Capacity in Man, by which he can dive into the Hearts of others, and know their most secret Thoughts with Certainty? *Alciph.* I don't think there is. *Euph.* When Actions are good and laudable in themselves, and there are two different Motives from which they might proceed, the one very honourable, and the other scandalous; which is it most charitable, to ascribe these Actions to the first Motive, or the latter? Why do you hesitate, *Alciphron*? Would not a polite Man, speaking to another's Face, say, that he thought his Actions proceeded from that Motive which does the most Honour to him? *Alciph.* I should think so. *Euph.* O *Alciphron*! from your own Concessions I can prove to you, how we ought to judge of *Nicanor*; and that it is highly injurious to ascribe his Industry, and the Pains he takes to get Money, to any Thing but his Love of Wine. The Minute Philosophers may say what they please; but Wine is not to be bought without Money; and you have own'd your self, that the more Money a Man has, the more he is able to buy Wine. These Things are self-evident: What a Man chuses, who is at Liberty to do what he pleases, he must prefer to that which he chuses not; and why should *Nicanor* drink Wine any more than he would eat Cheese, if he did not love it? That he drinks it, is plain; all his Friends and Acquaintance can testify it; they have been Eye-witnesses to it; therefore he loves it. And that he must love it beyond Measure, is plain; for he has forfeited his Reason for the Sake of it, and has drank Wine till he was drunk. *Alciphron* being silenced by the Force of these Arguments, *Lysicles* perhaps would say, that he could not give up this Point as *Alciphron* had done; but that he was not prepar'd to speak to it now, and therefore desired, that they might break off the Discourse. Thus *Euphranor* would triumph over his Adversary, and the Dialogue would end.

Duely to weigh these Two Characters, it is plain, that *Nicanor* was an abstemious Man; that the Motives which spurred him on to Industry, were his Love of Money, and Desire after worldly Greatness. Considering the small Delight he always seem'd to take in strong Liquors, and his known Thirst after Gain, it is impossible to account rationally for his excessive Drinking one Morning, than by ascribing it to his darling Passion, the Love of Lucre, which made him venture to lose his Sobriety rather than the Advantage which he expected from the Bargain he was driving. Therefore it is plain from this Character, that the Love of Wine, whether it was, counted blameable or praise-worthy, had no Influence upon *Nicanor*'s Actions, and consequently that, tho' it had been less than it was, it would never have diminish'd his Industry.

In *Lepidus* we see a fond Admirer of Company, and a discreet Lover of himself, who would enjoy as much of the World as is possible, without forfeiting the good Opinion of it: And a rich Man, of an even Temper, might perform all this in a Christian Country, from no better Principles than Pride and worldly Prudence, tho' he had very little or no Religion.

All This an hasty and inconsiderate Reader will call Folly, and tell me, that I am fighting with my own Shadow; and that, from the Character of *Nicanor*, no Mortal would imagine, that his Industry and Desire after Wealth could proceed from, and be owing to his Love of Wine: But I insist upon it, and you must allow it, Sir, that there would be no greater Absurdity in an Attempt of proving this, than there would be in ascribing the Sociableness and generous Behaviour of *Lepidus* to his being a Christian. All Men who are born of Christian Parents, and brought up among Christians, are always deem'd to be such themselves, whilst they acquiesce in, and not disown the Name: But unless People are palpably influenc'd by their Religion, in their Actions and Behaviour, there is no greater Advantage in being a Christian, than there is in being a Mahometan or a Heathen. If a Person was made free of a Company which presided over Artizans, in a toilsome laborious Trade, and he neither had serv'd his Time to it before, nor ever followed it afterwards, it could not be said of such a Person, whatever other Use he might make of his Freedom, that he actually was, or had been, of that laborious, toilsome Employment. A Man who was baptiz'd in his Infancy, may comply with all the outward Forms of his Religion; and, if he loves his Reputation, never be guilty of any notorious Wickedness. But if all this While, which is not impossible, his Heart is closely attach'd to this World; if he has a far greater Value for Sensual, than he has for Spiritual Pleasures, and persists in a Course of a voluptuous Life for many Years, without Repentance: A Man, I say, who does this, cannot be a more real Christian, tho' he conform'd to all the Rites and Ceremonies, and bore a great Sway in the Vestry, than a Linnen-Draper could be a real Blacksmith, tho' he was free of the Blacksmiths Company, and was a Livery-Man amongst them.

That weak silly People may form such wrong Judgments, as I have hinted at, from no worse Cause, than Want of Capacity, and mere Folly, I am willing to believe. But when I see Men of very good Sense, and considerable Knowledge, guilty of it, I can't help thinking, that they do it with Design, and because they find their Interest in it. This is certain, that when once it is taken for granted, that to be a Christian, it is sufficient to acquiesce in being call'd so, and attend the outward Worship of some Sect or other, it saves the Clergy a vast Deal of Trouble, from Friends as well as Foes. For to quiet and satisfy all scrupulous Consciences, is as great a Drudgery as it is to write in Defence of Miracles.

The Reason, Sir, why I have said so much on this Head, is, that among those who outwardly shew the greatest Zeal for Religion and the Gospel, I see hardly Any who teach us, either by Precept or Example, the Severity of Manners which Christianity requires. They seem to be much more sollicitous about the Name, than they are about the Thing it self; as if, when Men would but own themselves to be Christians, it was no great Matter for the Qualifications which must make them so. When of late I have cast my Eyes upon the Behaviour of some People, who shall be nameless, it has put me in

Mind of the *Free-Masons*. These, you know, are divided in several Companies; each Company have a Lodge of their own; every Lodge has a Master; over all these Masters again, there is a Grand Master. Some of them meet once a Month; others not so often; they pretend to Mysteries, and eat and drink together; they make use of several Ceremonies, which are peculiar to themselves, with great Gravity; and with all this Bustle they make, I could never learn yet, that they had any Thing to do, but to be *Free-Masons*, speak well of the Honour of their Society, and either pity or despise all those who are not Members of it: Out of their Assemblies, they live and converse like other Men: And tho' I have been in Company with several of them, I profess, unless I am told it, I can never know, who is a *Free-Mason*, and who is not.

I know, Sir, you love *Allegory*; and on that Score, I have been extremely delighted with what you say, Page 332, of your first Volume; where you justly ridicule and expose those Libertines, who pretend to be Patriots for *Liberty and Property*. I beg Leave, for the Benefit of other Readers, to transcribe the Passage. *When I hear, says Crito, these two Words in the Mouth of a* Minute Philosopher, *I am put in Mind of the* Teste di Ferro *at Rome. His Holiness, it seems, not having Power to assign Pensions, on* Spanish Benefices, *to Any but Natives of* Spain, *always keeps at* Rome *Two Spaniards, call'd* Teste di Ferro, *who have the Name of all such Pensions, but not the Profit, which goes to* Italians. *As we may see every Day, both Things and Notions placed to the Account of Liberty and Property, which in Reality neither have, nor are meant to have any Share in them. What! is it impossible for a Man to be a Christian, but he must be a Slave; or a Clergyman, but he must have the Principles of an Inquisitor?* This is very *à propos*, and admirably well applied. I thank you for it. I know Abundance of Divines, who seem to be very fond of the World, and are always grasping at Wealth and Power; and whenever I hear Any of these mention their Concern for Religion, and the Spiritual Welfare of Others, as they often do, I shall always think on *Crito*'s Story, laugh heartily, and say no more. For if I should imitate him, in exclaiming every Time I saw *both Things and Notions placed to the Account of* Religion and the Spiritual Welfare of Others, *which, in Reality, neither have, nor are meant to have any Share in them*, I should never be able to follow any other Business, than to cry out, What! is it impossible, that the Christian

Religion should be taken Care of, unless Ecclesiasticks ride in Coaches and Six; or the Spiritual Welfare of the Laity, without Temporal Dominion and an extravagant Power in the Clergy?

My *Allegory*, you see, Sir, is but a Copy of yours, and therefore cannot have the same Merit. How you will like it I can't tell; but I fancy, that most of my Readers besides, will be of Opinion, that if his Holiness makes no greater Advantage by his *Teste di Ferro* at *Rome*, than the Cause, which you espouse, is like to get by yours here, it will hardly be worth his while to keep them any longer.

Here, Sir, I shall take my Leave of you, in full Expectation, that, in what relates to me, I shall find great Alterations in your next Edition. To furnish you with as many Materials for this Purpose as I can conveniently, I shall fill what Room I have left with another Quotation from *The Fable of the Bees*, beginning Page 410. If my Paper would have held out, and I could have added a Page or two more, you would have seen how wickedly I have been misrepresented in what I say about the Fire of *London*.

It is certain, that the fewer Desires a Man has, and the less he Covets, the more easy he is to himself: The more active he is to supply his own Wants, and the less he requires to be waited upon, the more he will be beloved, and the less Trouble he is in a Family: The more he loves Peace and Concord, the more Charity he has for his Neighbour: And the more he shines in real Virtue, there is no doubt, but that in Proportion he is acceptable to God and Man. But let us be Just. What Benefit can these Things be of, or what Earthly Good can they do, to promote the Wealth, the Glory and Worldly Greatness of Nations? It is the Sensual Courtier, that sets no Limits to his Luxury; the Fickle Strumpet that invents New Fashions every Week; the Haughty Dutchess, that in Equipage, Entertainments, and all her Behaviour, would imitate a Princess; the Profuse Rake and lavish Heir, that scatter about their Money without Wit or Judgment, buy every Thing they see, and either destroy or give it away the next Day; the Covetous and perjur'd Villain, that squeez'd an immense Treasure from the Tears of Widows and Orphans, and left the Prodigals the Money to spend. It is these that are the Prey and proper Food of a full-grown Leviathan; or, in other Words, such is the calamitous Condition of Human Affairs, that we stand in Need of the Plagues and Monsters I named, to have all the Variety of Labour perform'd, which the Skill of Men is capable of inventing, in order to procure an Honest Livelihood to the vast Multitudes of Working Poor, that are required to make a large Society: And it is Folly to imagine, that great and wealthy Nations can subsist, and be at once Powerful and Polite, without.

I protest against Popery as much as ever Luther or Calvin did, or Queen Elizabeth herself; but I believe from my Heart, that the Reformation has, scarce been more instrumental in rendring the Kingdoms and States, that have embraced it, flourishing beyond other Nations, than the silly and capricious Invention of Hoop'd and Quilted Petticoats. But if this should be denied me by the Enemies of Priestly Power, at least I am sure, that, bar the brave Men, who have fought for and against that Lay-Man's Blessing, it has from its first Beginning to this Day, not employ'd so many Hands, honest industrious labouring Hands, as the abominable Improvement on Female Luxury, I named, has done in Few Years. Religion is one Thing, and Trade is another. He that gives most Trouble to Thousands of his Neighbours, and invents the most operose Manufactures is, right or wrong, the greatest Friend to the Society.

What a Bustle is there to be made in several Parts of the World, before a fine Scarlet, or Crimson Cloth can be produced? What a Multiplicity of Trades and Artificers must be employ'd? Not only such as are obvious, as Wool-combers, Spinners, the Weaver, the Cloth-worker, the Scowrer, the Dyer, the Setter, the Drawer, and the Packer; but others that are more remote, and might seem foreign to it; as the Mill-wright, the Pewterer, and the Chymist, which yet are all necessary, as well as a great Number of other Handicrafts, to have the Tools, Utensils, and other Implements belonging to the Trades already named: But all these Things are done at Home, and may be perform'd without extraordinary Fatigue or Danger; the most frightful Prospect is left behind, when we reflect on the Toil and Hazard that are to be undergone Abroad, the vast Seas we are to go over, the different Climates we are to endure, and the several Nations we must be obliged to for their Assistance. Spain alone, it is true, might furnish us with Wool to make the finest Cloth; but what Skill and Pains, what Experience and Ingenuity are required to dye it of those beautiful Colours! How widely are the Drugs and other Ingredients dispers'd through the Universe, that are to meet in one Kettle. Allom, indeed, we have of our own; Argol we might have from the Rhine, and Vitriol from Hungary; all this is in Europe; but then for Saltpetre in Quantity, we are forc'd to go as far as the East-Indies: Cochenille, unknown to the Ancients, is not much nearer to us, tho' in a quite different Part of the Earth; we buy it, 'tis true, from the Spaniards; *but not being their Product, they are forc'd to fetch it for us from the remotest Corner of the New World in the* West-Indies. *Whilst so many Sailors are broiling in the Sun, and swelter'd with Heat in the* East *and* West *of us, another Set of them are freezing in the* North, *to fetch Potashes from* Russia.

When we are thoroughly acquainted with all the Variety of Toil and Labour, the Hardships and Calamities, that must be undergone to compass the End I speak of, and we consider the vast Risques and Perils that are run in those Voyages, and that Few of them are ever made, but at the Expence, not only of the Health and Welfare, but even the Lives of Many: When we are acquainted with, I say and duely consider the Things I named, it is scarce possible to conceive a Tyrant so inhuman and void of Shame, that beholding Things in the same View, he should exact such terrible Services from his innocent Slaves; and at the same Time dare to own, that he did it for no other Reason, than the Satisfaction a Man receives from having a Garment made of Scarlet or Crimson Cloth. But to what Height of Luxury must a Nation be arriv'd, where not only the King's Officers, but likewise his Guards, even the Private Soldiers, should have such impudent Desires!

But if we turn the Prospect, and look on all those Labours, as so many voluntary Actions, belonging to different Callings and Occupations, that Men are brought up to for a Livelihood, and in which Every one works for himself, how much soever he may seem to labour for Others: If we consider, that even the Sailors, who undergo the greatest Hardships, as soon as one Voyage is ended, even after a Ship-wreck, are looking out and solliciting for Employment in another: If we consider, I say, and look on these Things in another View, we shall find, that the Labour of the Poor is so far from being a Burthen, and an Imposition upon them, that to have Employment is a Blessing, which, in their Addresses to Heaven, they pray for; and to procure it for the Generality of them, is the greatest Care of every Legislature.

FINIS.

PUBLICATIONS OF THE AUGUSTAN REPRINT SOCIETY

First Year (1946-47)

Numbers 1-6 out of print.

Second Year (1947-1948)

7. John Gay's *The Present State of Wit* (1711); and a section on Wit from *The English Theophrastus* (1702).

8. Rapin's *De Carmine Pastorali*, translated by Creech (1684).

9. T. Hanmer's (?) *Some Remarks on the Tragedy of Hamlet* (1736).

10. Corbyn Morris' *Essay towards Fixing the True Standards of Wit, etc.* (1744).

11. Thomas Purney's *Discourse on the Pastoral* (1717).

12. Essays on the Stage, selected, with an Introduction by Joseph Wood Krutch.

Third Year (1948-1949)

13. Sir John Falstaff (pseud.), *The Theatre* (1720).

14. Edward Moore's *The Gamester* (1753).

15. John Oldmixon's *Reflections on Dr. Swift's Letter to Harley* (1712); and Arthur Mainwaring's *The British Academy* (1712).

16. Nevil Payne's *Fatal Jealousy* (1673).

17. Nicholas Rowe's *Some Account of the Life of Mr. William Shakespeare* (1709).

18. "Of Genius," in *The Occasional Paper*, Vol. III, No. 10 (1719); and Aaron Hill's Preface to *The Creation* (1720).

Fourth Year (1949-1950)

19. Susanna Centlivre's *The Busie Body* (1709).

20. Lewis Theobold's *Preface to The Works of Shakespeare* (1734).

21. *Critical Remarks on Sir Charles Grandison, Clarissa, and Pamela* (1754).

22. Samuel Johnson's *The Vanity of Human Wishes* (1749) and Two *Rambler* papers (1750).

23. John Dryden's *His Majesties Declaration Defended* (1681).

24. Pierre Nicole's *An Essay on True and Apparent Beauty in Which from Settled Principles is Rendered the Grounds for Choosing and Rejecting Epigrams*, translated by J. V. Cunningham.

Fifth Year (1950-51)

25. Thomas Baker's *The Fine Lady's Airs* (1709).

26. Charles Macklin's *The Man of the World* (1792).

27. Frances Reynolds' *An Enquiry Concerning the Principles of Taste, and of the Origin of Our Ideas of Beauty, etc.* (1785).

28. John Evelyn's *An Apologie for the Royal Party* (1659); and *A Panegyric to Charles the Second* (1661).

29. Daniel Defoe's *A Vindication of the Press* (1718).

30. Essays on Taste from John Gilbert Cooper's *Letters Concerning Taste*, 3rd edition (1757), & John Armstrong's *Miscellanies* (1770).

Sixth Year (1951-1952)

31. Thomas Gray's *An Elegy Wrote in a Country Church Yard* (1751); and *The Eton College Manuscript.*

32. Prefaces to Fiction; Georges de Scudéry's Preface to *Ibrahim* (1674), etc.

33. Henry Gally's *A Critical Essay on Characteristic-Writings* (1725).

34. Thomas Tyers' A Biographical Sketch of Dr. Samuel Johnson (1785).

35. James Boswell, Andrew Erskine, and George Dempster. *Critical Strictures on the New Tragedy of Elvira, Written by Mr. David Malloch* (1763).

36. Joseph Harris's *The City Bride* (1696).

37. Thomas Morrison's *A Pindarick Ode on Painting* (1767).

38. John Phillips' *A Satyr Against Hypocrites.*

39. Thomas Warton's *A History of English Poetry.*

40. Edward Bysshe's *The Art of English Poetry.*

William Andrews Clark Memorial Library: University of California

The Augustan Reprint Society

General Editors

H. Richard Archer
Wm. Andrews Clark Memorial Library

Ralph Cohen
University of California, Los Angeles

R. C. Boys

Vinton A. Dearing

University of Michigan

University of California, Los Angeles

Corresponding Secretary: Mrs. Edna C. Davis, Wm. Andrews Clark Memorial Library

The Society exists to make available inexpensive reprints (usually facsimile reproductions) of rare seventeenth and eighteenth century works. The editorial policy of the Society remains unchanged. As in the past, the editors welcome suggestions concerning publications. All income of the Society is devoted to defraying cost of publication and mailing.

All correspondence concerning subscriptions in the United States and Canada should be addressed to the William Andrews Clark Memorial Library, 2205 West Adams Boulevard, Los Angeles 18, California. Correspondence concerning editorial matters may be addressed to any of the general editors. The membership fee is $3.00 a year for subscribers in the United States and Canada and 15/- for subscribers in Great Britain and Europe. British and European subscribers should address B. H. Blackwell, Broad Street, Oxford, England.

Publications for the seventh year [1952-1953]

(At least six items, most of them from the following list, will be reprinted.)

Selections from the Tatler, the Spectator, the Guardian. Introduction by Donald F. Bond.

Bernard Mandeville: *A Letter to Dion* (1732). Introduction by Jacob Viner.

M. C. Sarbiewski: *The Odes of Casimire* (1646), Introduction by Maren-Sofie Rœstvig.

An Essay on the New Species of Writing Founded by Mr. Fielding (1751). Introduction by James A. Work.

[Thomas Morrison]: *A Pindarick Ode on Painting* (1767). Introduction by Frederick W. Hilles.

[John Phillips]: *Satyr Against Hypocrits* (1655). Introduction by Leon Howard.

Prefaces to Fiction. Second series. Selected with an introduction by Charles Davies.

Thomas Warton: *A History of English Poetry: An Unpublished Continuation.* Introduction by Rodney M. Baine.

Publications for the first six years (with the exception of NOS. 1-6, which are out of print) are available at the rate of $3.00 a year. Prices for individual numbers may be obtained by writing to the Society.

THE AUGUSTAN REPRINT SOCIETY
WILLIAM ANDREWS CLARK MEMORIAL LIBRARY
2205 West Adams Boulevard, Los Angeles 18, California

Make check or money order payable to The Regents of the University of California.

Footnotes

1 In its only foreign language translation, the *Letter,* somewhat abbreviated, is appended to the German translation of *The Fable of the Bees* by Otto Bobertag, *Mandevilles Bienenfabel,* Munich, 1914, pp. 349-398.

2 Berkeley again criticized Mandeville in *A Discourse Addressed to Magistrates,* [1736], *Works,* A. C. Fraser ed., Oxford, 1871, III. 424.

3 *A Vindication of the Reverend D – – B – y,* London, 1734, applies to *Alciphron* the comment of Shaftesbury that reverend authors who resort to dialogue form may "perhaps, find means to laugh gentlemen into their religion, who have unfortunately been laughed out of it." See Alfred Owen Aldridge, "Shaftesbury and the Deist Manifes-

to," *Transactions of the American Philosophical Society*, New Series, XLI (1951), Part 2, p. 358.

⁴ Francis Hutcheson, a fellow-townsman of Berkeley, had previously made these points against Mandeville's treatment of luxury in letters to the *Dublin Journal* in 1726, (reprinted in Hutcheson, *Reflections upon Laughter, and Remarks upon the Fable of the Bees*, Glasgow, 1750, pp. 61-63, and in James Arbuckle, *Hibernicus' Letters*, London, 1729, Letter 46). In *The Fable of the Bees*, Mandeville concedes that gifts to charity would support employment as much as would equivalent expenditures on luxuries, but argues that in practice the gifts would not be made.

⁵ [Lord Hervey], *Some Remarks on the Minute Philosopher*, London, 1732, pp. 22-23, 42-50.

⁶ *Alciphron, or the Minute Philosopher*, T. E. Jessop, ed., in *The Works of George Berkeley, Bishop of Cloyne*. Edited by A. A. Luce and T. E. Jessop. London, etc., III. (1950), 9-10.

⁷ In his edition of *The Fable of the Bees*, Oxford, 1924, II. 415-416. All subsequent references to *The Fable of the Bees* will be to this edition.

⁸ *Fable of the Bees*, I. 48-49.

⁹ All page references placed in the main text of this introduction are to the *Letter to Dion*.

¹⁰ *Fable of the Bees*, II. 411. I, lxi, I, lvi.

¹¹ *Ibid.*, I. li, I. lv, I. cxxi.

[12] *Ibid.* I. cxxiv, note.

[13] For example, Kaye cites from Blewitt, a critic of Mandeville, this passage: "nothing can make a Man honest or virtuous but a Regard to *some* religious or moral Principles" and characterizes it as "precisely the rigorist position from which Mandeville was arguing when he asserted that our so-called virtues were really vices, because not based *only* on this regard to principle." (*Ibid.* II. 411. The italics in both cases are mine). The passage from Blewitt is not, of itself, manifestly rigoristic, while the position attributed to Mandeville is rigorism at its most extreme.

As further evidence of the prevalence of rigorism, Kaye cites from Thomas Fuller the following passage: "corrupt nature (which without thy restraining grace will have a Vent.)" *Ibid.* I. cxxi, note. But in Calvinist theology "restraining grace," which was not a "purifying" grace, operated to make some men who were not purged of sin lead a serviceable social life. (See John Calvin, *Institutes of the Christian Religion*, Bk. II, Ch. III, () 3, pp. I. 315-316 of the "Seventh American Edition," Philadelphia, n.d.) As I understand it, the role of "restraining grace" in Calvinist doctrine is similar to that of "honnêteté" in Jansenist doctrine, referred to *infra*. The rascals whom Mandeville finds useful to society are not to be identified either with those endowed with the "restraining grace" of the Calvinists or with the "honnêtes hommes" of the Jansenists.

For other instances of disregard by Kaye of the variations in substance and degree of the rigorism of genuine rigorists, see *ibid.* II. 403-406, II. 415-416.

[14] See especially F. B. Kaye, "The Influence of Bernard Mandeville," *Studies in Philology*, XIX (1922), 90-102.

¹⁵ Cf. Denziger-Bannwart, *Enchiridion Symbolorum.* (See index of any edition under "Baius," "Fénelon," "Iansen," "Iansenistae," "Quesnell.")

¹⁶ The most pertinent writings of Nicole for present purposes were his essays, "De la charité & de l'amour-propre," "De la grandeur," and "Sur l'évangile du Jeudi-Saint," which in the edition of his works published by Guillaume Desprez, Paris, 1755-1768, under the title *Essais de morale,* are to be found in volumes III, VI, and XI.

¹⁷ For a similar distinction by Bayle between *honnêtes hommes* who are not of the elect and the outright rascals, see Pierre Bayle, *Dictionaire historique et critiqué.* 5th ed., Amsterdam, 1740, "Éclaircissement sur les obscénités," IV. () iv, p. 649.

¹⁸ *Fable of the Bees,* I. 19.

¹⁹ In the French versions of 1740 and 1750, the title, *The Fable of the Bees: or, Private Vices, Publick Benefits,* is translated as *La fable des abeilles ou les fripons devenus honnestes gens.*

For the "honnête homme" in 17th and 18th century usage as intermediate between a knave and a saint, see M. Magendie, *La politesse mondaine et les théories de l'honnêteté en France,* Paris, n.d., (ca. 1925), and William Empson, *The Structure of Complex Words,* London, 1951, ch. 9, "Honest Man."

²⁰ Kaye in a note to this parable, *Fable of the Bees,* I. 238, cites as relevant, *I Cor. x. 31;* "Whether therefore ye eat, or drink, or whatsoever ye do, do all to the glory of God." Even more relevant, I believe, is *Deut. xxix. 19,* where, in the King James version, the sinner boasts: "I shall have peace, though I walk in the imagination of mine heart, to add drunkenness to thirst."

[21] "Pensées diverses sur la foi, et sur les vices opposés," *Oeuvres de Bourdaloue*, Paris, 1840, III. 362-363.

[22] John Plamenatz, *The British Utilitarians*, Oxford and New York, 1949, pp. 48-49.

[23] Helvétius, *De l'esprit*, Discours II. Ch. XXIV. In the French version of *The Fable of the Bees*, the phrasing is almost identical: See *La fable des abeilles*, Paris, 1750, e.g. II. 261: "ménagés avec dextérité par d'habiles politiques." When the Sorbonne, in 1759, condemned *De l'esprit*, it cited *The Fable of the Bees* as among the works which could have inspired it. (F. Grégoire. *Bernard De Mandeville*, Nancy, 1947, p. 206).

Kaye, in his "The Influence of Bernard Mandeville," (*loc. cit.*, p. 102), says that *De l'esprit* "Is in many ways simply a French paraphrase of *The Fable*." In his edition of *The Fable of the Bees*, however, he says, "I think we may conclude no more than that Helvétius had probably read *The Fable*." (*Fable of the Bees*, I. CXLV, Note). Kaye systematically fails to notice the significance of Mandeville's emphasis on the rôle of the "skilful Politician."

[24] *Mr. Dennis.*

[25] *Dr. Fiddes's Treatise of Morality, Pref. Page XIX.*